KOOCH N. DANIELS, MA

STARS, CARDS, AND STONES

Exploring Cosmic Connections between Astrology, Tarot, and Runestones

4880 Lower Valley Road, Atglen, PA 19310

Library of Congress Control Number: 2024932771

Designed by Brenda McCallum
Production design by Alexa Harris
Cover design by Brenda McCallum

Cover images: denbelitsky/Bigstock; Bigc Studio/Bigstock; Olga Soloveva/Shutterstock
Interior image: p. 11, Romolo Tavani/Shutterstock
Type set in Fenice BT/Times New Roman/New Frank

ISBN: 978-0-7643-6840-0
978-1-5073-0405-1 (Epub)
Printed in China

Published by REDFeather Mind, Body, Spirit
An imprint of Schiffer Publishing, Ltd.
4880 Lower Valley Road
Atglen, PA 19310
Phone: (610) 593-1777; Fax: (610) 593-2002
Email: Info@redfeathermbs.com
Web: www.redfeathermbs.com

For our complete selection of fine books on this and related subjects, please visit our website at www.schifferbooks.com. You may also write for a free catalog.

REDFeather Mind, Body, Spirit's titles are available at special discounts for bulk purchases for sales promotions or premiums. Special editions, including personalized covers, corporate imprints, and excerpts, can be created in large quantities for special needs. For more information, contact the publisher.

We are always looking for people to write books on new and related subjects. If you have an idea for a book, please contact us at proposals@schifferbooks.com.

Disclaimer. The material within this book is not intended to be used as treatment for any form of psychological or physical disorder. The author or publisher makes no claims or takes any responsibility for healing problems. When using the information provided in relation to the oracles, the author advises novice readers, professional readers, and licensed practitioners of counseling and healing arts to work within the framework of their expertise. It's also recommended that readers of this book acquire additional resources to study stars, cards, and stones, since there's always more to learn.

These words sparkle with star bright thanks to my supernova gems, Victor, Tara, Lila, Chris, Bailey & Hailey, who shine the light of inspiration on my path.

ENDORSEMENTS

"Having had the pleasure of working with Kooch in her capacity as a reader and teacher in the divinatory arts for many years, I can freely express my admiration for her energy, wisdom, and willingness to explore the frontiers of spirit. Be it palmistry, astrology, Tarot, runes, or any one of several disciplines, her skill, compassion, and devotion to giving her best in every circumstance is truly inspirational. Her wide-ranging, frequently eclectic, knowledge base deepens what she brings to every class she teaches, every book she writes, and every reading table she joins."

—Thalassa, event producer & divinista, oracular readings, instruction, and events, www.dodivination.com

"Kooch Daniels is an 'opti-mystic intuitive' whose inner sight into symbols, images, and runes demystifies the hidden treasures deep inside each of us. Her ability to help us see our own inner magic is also one of her unique skills."

—Jeanne M. House, editor of *Peak Vitality: Raising the Threshold of Abundance in Our Material, Spiritual, and Emotional Lives*

"A lifetime of experience and passion pours into this book. Kooch Daniels has been an inspiration sharing her knowledge of the hidden mysteries to her readers. I look forward to taking a deep dive into this work. It has a spot on the 'Top Shelf' in my library."

—Peter Coe, Peter Michael Practical Tarot

"Kooch Daniels, MA, is a popular and professional intuitive that has created another original book, *Stars, Cards, and Stones*. The student will learn to work with ancient oracles, astrology, Tarot, and runestones. The reader, through discussions of traditional chart interpretation, can improve their lives as well as others while building a foundation with zodiac templates and cards and runestones. This brilliant author has published an array of books to aide any student in the mystical realm.

—Jeane Slone, local-authors distributor and author of four historical novels

"I have known Kooch Daniels for fifty years, during which she has continuously developed her skills as a psychic reader and teacher. In this book, she integrates the three divination techniques of astrology, the Tarot, and the runes into a comprehensive system that provides far more information about life decisions than any one of the techniques could do by itself. This book will teach you how to use this ingenious system for yourself and for others. I highly recommend it."

—Aidan A. Kelly, PhD, professor of theology and religious history, Cherry Hill Seminary

CONTENTS

ACKNOWLEDGMENTS

Most importantly, I would like to thank Pete Schiffer, who is giving my manuscript a home. Christopher McClure, who had been the fearless leader of the REDFeather Mind, Body, Spirit division of Schiffer, has my heartfelt gratitude and appreciation for accepting my work and believing in my vision. I also want to thank my editor, Peggy Kellar, for her positive energy and excellence and also give a hearty round of applause to the helping hands of Schiffer's design team who put their magic into making this book come to life.

I especially want to thank Geri De Stefano Webre, Alta Picchi, and Judy Blake, my early Tarot teachers, who gifted me with countless hours of classes, support, and guidance. Our time spent together opened the door for learning to trust my intuition and working as an intuitive. And a heart full of thanks is being sent to Ralph Blum and Deon Dolphin, both of whom introduced me to the rune mysteries while we all were readers at the California Renaissance Faire.

Dr. Eleanor Criswell, who bravely supervised a Tarot counseling center on my college campus many decades ago, is due a large round of applause for her trailblazing bravery to go where other professors feared to tread. Down the same long corridor, I had the privilege to study Jungian and archetypal psychology with Gordon Tappan, who will always be the magician, the hero, and the wise old man in my eyes.

The first person to read my manuscript was Aiden Kelly, pagan author and professor of religion, who was one of the founding members of the New Reformed Order of the Golden Dawn in the San Francisco Bay area in the late '60s. Like a true sage, he graciously offered his editing critiques.

I count my blessings for my star-aligned partner, Victor Daniels, who is willing to read and discuss my text with loving support. Also, I can never give enough thanks to Cris Wanzer for her editing expertise and encouragement for my efforts. Much appreciation also goes to Lila Burke and Maureen O'Sullivan for reading some of my text when I asked for their insights.

Not surprisingly, there aren't enough words to thank all the wonderful artists who have granted me permission to use their art, and the generosity of Schiffer Publishing Company for letting me use their illustrations within these pages. Tarot artists are Cathy McClelland, Beth Seilonen, Pamela Steele, Anna Franklin, Yasmeen Westwood, Ciro Marchetti, Gina Thies, Steven Bright, Marie White, Dinah Roseberry, Miriam Jacobs, J. R. Rivera, Jasmine Becket Griffith, and Robert Place.

Also, my appreciation goes to Thomas Michael Caldwell for sharing his Nordic wisdom and his poem "The Ancient Runes," and Mark Murphy for his rune-Tarot images. My heartfelt thanks goes to Tara Daniels, who helped me photograph my runes.

My infinite appreciation goes to all astrology, Tarot, and rune muses and masters whose teachings illuminate the oracular path. And I can never give enough thanks to my mystical guides, Vedic scholar Harish Johari and India's loving, hugging saint, Mata Amritanandamayi.

It's impossible to thank all the people who have trusted me to give them readings, for how could my skills grow if I couldn't draw on the vibrant slates of their perceptions? And what kind of person might I be if I didn't mention you, and all my readers who give me reason to write these words? From my heart, loving thanks to all.

Artists and Contributors

My deepest gratitude goes to the following deck creators who enlighten my pages with their beautiful art. Their permission to use their bold images has brought visual inspiration to my discussions. I'm listing each artist with their Tarot card titles listed beneath their name. Images are courtesy of

Jasmine Becket-Griffith, illustrator and her collaborator and author
J. R. Rivera, *Beautiful Creatures Tarot*
Chapter 5: 19. The Sun
Chapter 7: 10. The Wheel

Steven Bright, *Spirit within Tarot*
Chapter 7: 12. The Hanged Man
15. The Devil

Anna Franklin, *Pagan Ways Tarot*
Chapter 7: 1. The Magician
6. The Lovers
14. Temperance
Chapter 9: 10. Wyrd

Miriam Jacobs, *Polarity Wellness Tarot*
Chapter 7: 22. The Fool

Ciro Marchetti, *The Mystic Palette Tarot*
Chapter 7: 3. The Empress

Cathy McClelland, *The Star Tarot*
Chapter 7: 5. The Hierophant, a.k.a. The High Priest
7. Chariot
8. Strength

Robert M. Place, *The Alchemical Tarot: Renewed* (4th Edition)
Chapter 7: 20. Judgement
And *The Tarot of the Sevenfold Mystery*
Chapter 7: 9. The Hermit
21. The World

Dinah Roseberry, *First Light Tarot*
The Star: NASA, ESA, and P. Kalas (University of California, Berkeley, USA)
Chapter 7: 17. The Star

Beth Seilonen, *Dream Raven Tarot*
Chapter 7: 11. Justice

Pamela Steel, *The Eternal Oracle*
Part 2, Introduction
Odin's Wheel
Chapter 7: 9. Hermit

Gina G. Thies, *Tarot of the Moors*
Chapter 7: 4. The Sultan (The Emperor)
19. The Sun

Yasmeen Westwood, *Enchanted Dreams*
Chapter 7: 2. The High Priestess
16. The Tower

Marie White, *Mary-El Tarot*
Part 1, Introduction – 3. The Empress
Chapter 7: 13. Death
18. The Moon

Other artistic contributors

Tara Daniels
Photos of runestones

Mark Murphy
Images of runes with cards

Thomas Michael Caldwell
Chapter 5, The poem "The Ancient Runes"

FOREWORD

Some of the oldest questions in the history of humankind, with or without words, have been

"What's going to happen to me?"

"How can I best survive?"

"Where can we live?"

People sought ways to answer questions such as these even before writing was invented. They looked everywhere for answers. They looked at the stars to see whether their movements and alignments offered any insights, and at the ground to see if the twigs and stones held clues to ease their uncertainties.

Move forward into the mists of time, and then, in the 1400s, someone created Tarot cards, which told a story with every drawing. Many of the cards were drawn with constellations that could be used as references for discussions.

Stars and cards each had their seers and sleuths who could see certain regularities in the messages that each seemed to hold. Some of these seers, and others, including readers of stones and twigs, had remarkable insight—especially if they attended not just to messages in the stars, but also to what they could fathom on the surface and in the depths of those who came for forecasts and advice.

As time marched forward into the twentieth century, psychologists—healers and would-be healers of the mind and heart, with letters after their name and certificates on the wall—assumed the leading role as those who could give insight into complexities of mind and heart. The star, card, and stone readers went behind closed doors, and there was no more need for the seers of the old ways, right?

Surprise! Demand for the readers did not fall from public interest. Seers offered a different kind of experience than people had in counseling and psychotherapy. And even a few psychologists learned to use the cards, and a few readers added to their repertoire by studying psychology and even getting letters behind their names. Kooch is one of those who did so, immersing herself in archetypes and Jungian psychology. She's also one of the few who dedicated her life to the ancient oracles. She's a lifelong Tarot reader, an astrologer who watches the movements of stars and planets, and the interpreter of numerous bags of runestones. She has the skill to dance back and forth from one oracle to another and fathom the ways in which each of these oracles can inform the others.

Kooch has come a long way from her youthful days when she sat in San Francisco's Ghirardelli Square and did readings for a dollar each. Of course, a dollar bought more in those days—and afforded her a priceless initiation into the world of divination.

No one else I know has combined all three of these classical divinatory systems into one voice. Beyond knowing about each of them, Kooch can draw on her knowledge of how to do a reading combining all three of them that can blow your mind. In these pages she shows you how you can do that too.

—Victor Daniels, PhD
emeritus professor, Sonoma State University;
consultant, author, and workshop leader

PART ONE

INTRODUCTION

A CELESTIAL GATEWAY TO DIVINATION

MYSTICAL MUSINGS

A warm autumn wind whispered through the oaks that shaded the many booths in Witches Woods—an area at the end of a leaf-strewn earthen path that meandered through the Renaissance Pleasure Faire just north of San Francisco. People sat in line on hay bales waiting for a reading, hoping their questions, great and small, would soon be answered.

A woman in her thirties, with eyes as blue as her Elizabethan gown, sat across from me. "Do the cards tell whether I have a future with my boyfriend?" she asked. She smiled shyly, obviously hoping the answer would be yes. "We enjoy each other and our intimacy, but he never says anything about our future and starts getting nervous if I do. He was married for six years and says it hurt him badly when his wife left unexpectedly and never told him why. I think he's afraid to get too close to anyone again. Is that true or is it just me?"

The final or resolution card in her spread was the third Major Arcana card, The Empress, linked with Venus, the goddess of love, nurturing, and compassion. Because of this card's auspicious significance, I hinted that her romance was moving in a positive direction and might turn out well.

Her eyes smiled, but her self-doubt made it hard for her to believe the card could be right. After all, if she got her hopes up, they might be painfully dashed.

"Can we try the runes also?" she asked, pointing to my nearby stones.

I obliged, opened my Nordic cloth, and invited her to throw the stones. She hesitated, then picked them up and fiercely tossed them across my table. The overseeing muses continued their dialogue, silently speaking through various upward-facing runes.

"What do they say?" she asked.

I saw instantly that they were an uncanny reflection of the Tarot spread, but I left her to a moment of tense anticipation while I continued to fathom their message. Then I nodded slightly and said, "The stone that represents your potential direction is Beorc, associated with Venus, the planet of fertility and sensuality, and Freyja, Norse goddess of love and sorcery. Since the Empress card and this stone honor the blossoming of passion, both of your readings show a rich potential to find happiness. The runes don't say for certain that you'll find it with this partner, but they certainly suggest that it's worth persevering with your relationship to find out."

Years later, the memory of this reading and others like it developed into the recurring theme that astrology can play an equal role in the interpretation both of Tarot cards and runestones. When I've offered readings that combine these divinatory arts, their messages usually reinforce each other through shared archetypal themes and universal symbols. My decades of doing readings in settings ranging from colorful fairs to corporate parties, and for querents who range from the rich to those down on their luck, became the inspiration for this guide to explain how the stars, cards, and stones connect.

When you can communicate using the star power of astrology, you have the knowledge to speak a symbolic language that runs through other esoteric mediums. Without studying the conceptual framework of the Tarot and runes, you may not understand how to transfer this knowledge, but you have it. As you learn the celestial connections these mystical arts share, your ability to create useful interpretations based on their comparable keywords and themes can grow quickly.

Once considered a science, astrology has been used throughout history to help with inner understanding of life's outer complexities. A primary root supporting the tree of divination, it can also illuminate hidden meanings encoded on the cards and stones. The more you understand basic astrology, the more easily you'll be able to unveil the secrets and significance of each card and stone.

When viewed as a cosmic calendar, astrology's precise measurements of time can be used to contemplate how one might best move through life, navigate challenges, and awaken a higher sense of worldly and spiritual purpose. As you search its vivid imagery for clues to patterns of thinking, feeling, and acting—in each moment and also larger life cycles—you open your mind knowingly or unknowingly to the realm of archetypal possibilities.

Carl Jung described archetypes as the universal patterns, themes, and qualities reflected within the psyche that are timelessly played out in the conscious and unconscious collective minds of humanity.[1] When you light the lamp of astrological wisdom, you also open a portal to viewing these shared conceptional patterns. Every zodiac sign and planet, every Major Arcana card, and every runestone is linked with an archetype. Understanding archetypal symbols in the zodiac is like having a magic compass that points to the shared potentials, the secrets, and the messages within the stars, cards, and runestones.

As you journey through these pages, you'll be invited to explore the parallel connections and possibilities interwoven among these symbolic arts. You'll also learn how you can use the wheel of the zodiac for creating card spreads and rune casts.

AS YOU JOURNEY AROUND THE SUN

Just as you can gaze at the moon on a bright starry night, you can fashion an astrological design to chart Tarot and runestone correspondences. To have success with the method offered in this text, it's important to learn the basic, key features on the wheel of the zodiac. A working knowledge of these features makes it possible to view the cards and stones from a celestial perspective.

When traveling the mystic trail, it's usually best to allow your intuition and common sense to dialogue with one another. Balance your head and your heart to find answers that point to sensible ways to handle choices you might need to make. When working with any oracle, be alert to what practices work best for you, so you'll have the greatest opportunity to find success (they might or might not be the same ones that work best for someone else).

While contemplating connections among the stars, cards, and stones, you may notice there are many different pathways to guide you—probably more than you'll ever have time to take. You can study them in relation to mythology, philosophy, alchemy, archetypes, or specific cultures in history. You can even find them linked with religious traditions and realms of fantasy that may be of special personal interest to you. In these pages I've focused on astrology's all-embracing themes, the obvious and hidden messages, the conscious and unconscious dimensions, and their connections with themes that can be found in the ancient well of stories about their relevance in awakening new potentials for developing your psychic abilities.

As you study the history of these popular oracular practices, you might find yourself thinking that these three systems are not created equal. You're right! Each began in a different part of the world, at different times, and their associated mythologies were shaped by distinctive cultures. The societies in which runes originated worshiped the Germanic, Celtic, Norse, and Viking gods. Tarot scholars link their beginnings with Zoroastrianism and Roman, Greek, or Egyptian deities. In the past, before the printing press, Tarot cards were hard to find, but now they're ubiquitous. In runic history, everyone had access to stones, bones, and twigs upon which the runes were engraved. Today, most people living in cities don't have easy access to nature and find it easier to use book stores or online sources for their rune craft supplies.

Despite their differences, astrology, Tarot cards, and runestones are similar in many ways. Voiced in the silent language of symbols that stretch beyond time and culture, each can reveal transcendent wisdom and offer insight into recurring patterns existing in the collective subconscious. The sign of the sun in 3000 BCE has much the same luminous, positive meaning as in 2024 CE. Honored throughout time, its pictogram or image inspires a sense of the life-giving, renewing power delivered in waves of radiant light.

All in-depth explorations of symbols, especially astrological ones, touch on the unity and interconnectedness of human experience in one way or another. A psychological or philosophical exploration of their qualities can take us on an incredible journey into the depths of the known and unknown mysteries hidden within path-worn labyrinths of sacred temples where truth resides.

Even if you don't want to memorize key correlations, don't underestimate the value of learning the traditional astrological meanings that have been agreed upon and endlessly repeated throughout the ages. Once you grasp the basic concepts, you've gone through a cosmic growth spurt that can help you make sense of things that might otherwise seem mysterious. This includes interpreting symbols on a horoscope, seeing how signs of the zodiac can enrich your understanding of how to read cards or stones, or using sun signs and planets as metaphors to shed light on the human psyche.

Also, when you can discuss the values attributed to the symbols associated with the signs and planets, you possess the knowledge that is needed to interpret their corresponding cards and stones. If your goal is to do readings, once you understand astrological connecting points with other mystical mediums, the vastness of psychic space moves closer within reach, and you will have acquired a principal resource for building a successful divination practice.

To begin this study, the first step is increasing your awareness of the symbolic language found on the Wheel of the Zodiac. The next is believing in the wisdom of your intuitive self and turning this page.

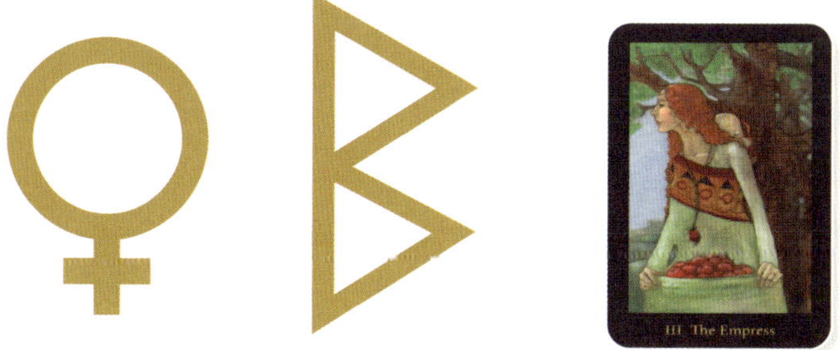

The planet Venus + the rune Beorc + the major card The Empress
Each shares the qualities of love, beauty, and joy.

CHAPTER 1

BUILDING YOUR ASTROLOGICAL FOUNDATION

The twinkling stars of the nighttime sky have fascinated humankind throughout history. From ancient times to the present, stargazers have searched the constellations to find answers to questions about how planetary movements influence the cloaked mysteries of life. Historically, the stars have been viewed by many as guiding lights that help humanity navigate uncharted space and time, and their visual study has been used to expand the understanding of our collective unconscious and conscious minds. One of the more famous stars, the Star of Bethlehem, was revered by seers for announcing the birth of Christ. Sirius, the Dog Star, also known as the Star of Isis, has been studied for its influence on the fluctuating tides of the Nile. Many other stars and their constellations, venerated for their brilliance, are personified with characteristics shared with the gods and goddesses in early mythologies.

Astrology, not to be confused with astronomy, which is tethered to the roots of science, often relates to the study of the multifaceted components of the personality. When used in such a manner, star formations and positions become virtual maps for highlighting challenges and opportunities in the wide-ranging scope of existence. From within this long-established framework, we'll look at how the stars can also shine on attributes of the cards and stones, including their archetypal potentials.

Works exploring the history of civilization tell us that astrology has been with us nearly as long as written history. The constellations and the planets sitting within them have been recorded in ancient Phoenicia, Babylon, Chaldea, Greece, India, and China, as well as other culturally rich territories. Runic cultures are known to have viewed the stars and planets through strategic points in their stone megaliths, which were aligned with the ticking clock of nature's planetary rhythms. In the Middle Ages, royalty and high-ranking officials, before making major decisions, are said to have consulted with astrologers. During the Renaissance, astrology was studied in college as a natural science. Throughout the portals of time, zodiacal calculations have been reputed to foreshadow the direction of events, offer clues to the secrets of human nature, and illuminate the truth within.

In modern times, star-minded people continue to use astrology in hopes of finding some certainty in an uncertain future, and to search for clarity concerning life's direction and purpose. Before the technological age, astrologers used their knowledge of the position of the planets and spent a long time creating a person's horoscope. Today, with the popularity of computers and their quick computations, within minutes a person can generate and print out a horoscope. The most common of these is the natal chart, which is a circular diagram divided into twelve houses that reflect the cosmic potential of one's unique, earthly journey. These charts show where the planets were located in the heavens at the exact moment of someone's birth. Once a chart is constructed, the person who understands its symbols has the means to examine and analyze the complexities of life through its planetary positions. Even though the study of a chart is not limited to character analysis and probabilities, its examination is typically used to uncover the mystery of the self and one's unfolding capabilities and purpose.

Different stargazers speak about sun signs and the planets in different ways. People living in various cultures view the cosmic movements from their unique perspectives. For example, the Chinese use animal symbols, such as the dragon, snake, and the boar, to mark certain movements on the zodiac wheel. The Mayan astrological system uses five elements instead of four, and they have twenty sun signs. If you adopt Vedic astrology, you'll learn a method based on Vedic philosophy of ancient India. Although these systems are different from the Western astrological perspective, they all possess insight into the rhythmic beat of the outer world of relationships and the inner measure of personality, patterns, and potentials.

The starting point for the beginning student is to learn about the essential components of the zodiac—the sun signs, the planets, the elements, and the houses. This study will guide you in laying the foundation you need to analyze a chart and discuss questions concerning personal growth, self-knowledge, the karmic forces of cause and effect, and your divinatory know-how. Learning this information is also important for being able to do the card spreads and rune casts discussed in later pages. You also have an additional opportunity to learn more about the qualities of each of the sun signs and the planets in part 3, "The Mystical Library."

THE TWELVE SUN SIGNS

The zodiac is a brilliant ring of constellations that the sun, moon, and planets appear to move through during each year as the earth circles the sun. Like all the stars, these constellations don't stand still relative to the spinning earth but appear to rotate around us during each cycle of night and day. Around five thousand years ago, the Sumerians divided this band into twelve signs, each representing 30 degrees of space. Each sign was named after the most prominent constellation in that part of the band. Although there is debate concerning the Babylonian versus Sumerian naming of the sun signs, the following names and their dates are those used in Western astrology:

The Sun Signs	Dates
Aries, the Ram	March 21–April 20
Taurus, the Bull	April 21–May 20
Gemini, the Twins	May 21–June 20
Cancer, the Crab	June 21–July 20
Leo, the Lion	July 21–Aug. 20
Virgo, the Virgin	Aug. 21–Sept. 20
Libra, the Scales	Sept. 21–Oct. 20
Scorpio, the Scorpion	Oct. 21–Nov. 20
Sagittarius, the Archer	Nov. 21–Dec. 20
Capricorn, the Goat	Dec. 21–Jan. 20
Aquarius, the Water Bearer	Jan. 21–Feb. 20
Pisces, the Fish	Feb. 21–March 20

About 2,500 to 3,000 years ago, the Babylonians divided the circle of the zodiac into 360 degrees. They defined each sign as covering 30 degrees of arc in the sky, making the zodiac appear as a wheel with twelve equal spokes. Each sun sign was seen as an expression of natural forces related to the conditions of human life. Many of their influences were described in comparison to the attributes of the gods or goddesses that were revered in relation to the energy of the sun's light when coming through specific constellations. These characteristics have been passed on through the portals of time by all those who have influenced the meanings assigned to the signs and planets as we understand them today. If you're planning to interpret astrology charts, you'll need to know the twelve sun signs, their natural order, and their principal qualities. To help you become familiar with the twelve signs, the following list offers some of their time-honored associations:

GETTING TO KNOW THE SUN SIGNS

Ruler:	Mars
Phrase:	I am
House:	First
Quality:	Cardinal
Element:	Fire
Body:	Head
Gem:	Coral

Ruler:	Venus
Phrase:	I have
House:	Second
Quality:	Fixed
Element:	Earth
Body:	Throat, Neck
Gem:	Emerald

Ruler:	Mercury
Phrase:	I think
House:	Third
Quality:	Mutable
Element:	Air
Body:	Lungs, nerves, hands
Gem:	Aquamarine, tourmaline

Ruler:	Moon
Phrase:	I feel
House:	Fourth
Quality:	Cardinal
Element:	Water
Body:	Breasts, chest, stomach
Gem:	Pearl, Moonstone

Ruler:	Sun
Phrase:	I will
House:	Fifth
Quality:	Fixed
Element:	Fire
Body:	Heart, upper back
Gem:	Ruby

Ruler:	Mercury
Phrase:	I analyze
House:	Sixth
Quality:	Mutable
Element:	Earth
Body:	Intestines, bowels
Gem:	Jasper

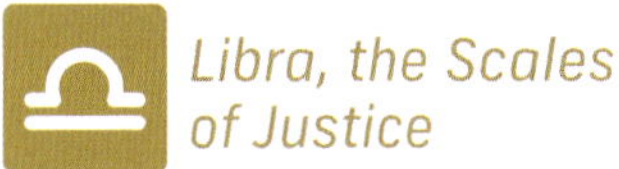

Libra, the Scales of Justice

Ruler:	Venus
Phrase:	I balance
House:	Seventh
Quality:	Cardinal
Element:	Air
Body:	Kidney, lower back
Gem:	Opal, peridot

Scorpio, the Scorpion

Rulers:	Mars and Pluto
Phrase:	I desire
House:	Eighth
Quality:	Fixed
Element:	Water
Body:	Reproductive organs, bladder
Gem:	Topaz

Sagittarius, the Archer

Ruler:	Jupiter
Phrase:	I see
House:	Ninth
Quality:	Mutable
Element:	Fire
Body:	Thighs, hips
Gem:	Lapis lazuli

Capricorn, the Goat

Ruler:	Saturn
Phrase:	I utilize
House:	Tenth
Quality:	Cardinal
Element:	Earth
Body:	Knees, skeleton, teeth
Gem:	Onyx, hematite

Aquarius, the Water Bearer

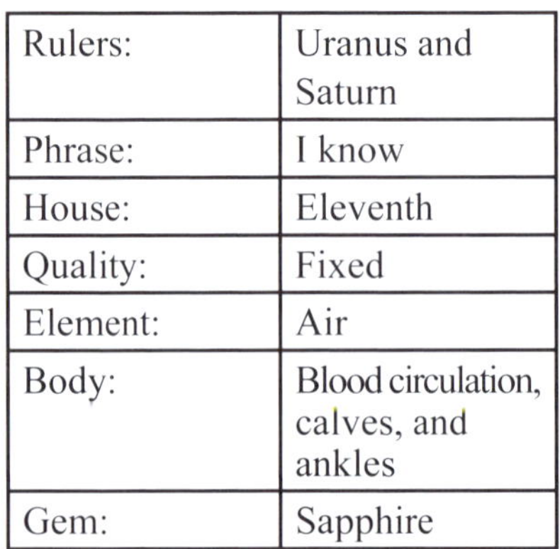

Rulers:	Uranus and Saturn
Phrase:	I know
House:	Eleventh
Quality:	Fixed
Element:	Air
Body:	Blood circulation, calves, and ankles
Gem:	Sapphire

Pisces, the Fish

Rulers:	Jupiter and Neptune
Phrase:	I believe
House:	Twelfth
Quality:	Mutable
Element:	Water
Body:	Feet, toes
Gem:	Amethyst

The Wheel of the Zodiac

Each sun sign is associated with one of the four elements: fire, earth, air, or water. Clues to the underlying nature of each sign can be found in the qualities associated with its governing element. Our initial exploration begins with viewing their fundamental components, the elements.

THE FOUR ELEMENTS

Since early times, it had been expressed in Western cultures that matter consisted of the four elements of fire, earth, air, and water, combined in various proportions. Because astrology was originally taught in school as a science, its proponents began to draw comparisons between the elements and the fundamental features of consciousness mapped out on the zodiac wheel. By the fifth century, correlations between the sun signs and the elements became an established aspect of western astrology.

With observation, you'll notice that the elements as they sit within the horoscope always occur in the sequence of fire, earth, air, and water. The following descriptions list some of their time-honored connections:

Fire governs high-spirited Aries, Leo, and Sagittarius. This element indicates high energy within the spirit of fiery, active, motivated, creative, and enterprising personalities.

Earth influences the rooted, practical energy of Capricorn, Taurus, and Virgo. The earth element corresponds to the body and practical, productive, tangible, or financial energies.

Air rules the signs Libra, Aquarius, and Gemini. Air equals thinking and the world of ideas, mediating dualities and challenging communications, and the networking of people and businesses.

Water is associated with Cancer, Scorpio, and Pisces. Water flows with strong emotions and a keen sensitivity to vibrations and intuitive feelings.

Element	Polarity	Sun Sign Partners	Tendency
Fire	Positive	Aries, Leo, and Sagittarius	Activates
Earth	Negative	Capricorn, Taurus, and Virgo	Moderates
Air	Positive	Libra, Aquarius, and Gemini	Penetrates
Water	Negative	Cancer, Scorpio, and Pisces	Embraces

Every chart has an interplay of influences in relation to some combination of these four elements. For example, one person's chart may contain several planets sitting in the sign Leo, associated with the element of fire, positive-high energy, and an extroverted nature. Another person may have five planets, called a preponderance (majority of one element), sitting in the house of Scorpio, linked with water, strong emotions, and the occult. You might surmise that your client is an intuitive person who flows with his or her moods because of the predominance of water in his or her chart. Or, you may see that someone's chart has a complete absence of an element. Sometimes a person will develop the qualities that are missing on their chart by becoming involved with these elements through their interactions with others. For instance, if a person doesn't have any planets sitting in signs rooted in the earth element, he or she may not be grounded. They may find themselves attracting practical-minded friends who possess potent earth energies and have an enterprising nature.

Signs have positive/negative or yang/yin polarities in connection to their corresponding element. Sun signs that share positive energy are those governed by the elements of fire and air: Aries, Gemini, Leo, Libra, Sagittarius, and Aquarius. These are said to be extroverted and outwardly expressive. The signs that share a negative polarity are those tied to the elements of water and earth: Cancer, Scorpio, Pisces, Taurus, Virgo, and Capricorn. They're often characterized as introverted and private minded. Elements can be discussed symbolically or literally. How do you view them manifesting in your life? Through your personal experience of the nature of elements, you can gain insight into their many qualities and learn to identify their basic values. How do you see the elements interacting with one another in your personal experiences? For instance, how might you compare the abundant flow of emotions (water) when feeling happy compared to an inflamed sense of feeling anger (fire)? Imagine the differences between water bubbling in a fountain and water that has turned into frozen ice on a winter's night. How do your feelings compare the experience of watching a fire at a campsite and watching a movie with a fiery actress in a heated love scene?

Keywords for the Four Elements

Element	Governs	Power	Skill	Influences
Fire	Spirit	Actions	Creativity	Asserting
Water	Emotions	Flows	Receptivity	Feelings
Air	Intellect	Soars	Focusing	Thinking
Earth	Body	Secures	Grounding	Touching

If, during your studies, you read that there are five elements, don't become alarmed. The fifth element, known as Ether (called Akasha in Sanskrit), is predominant in Eastern yoga and Vedic philosophic discussions. It represents a field of invisible, weightless energy encompassing the emptiness of space. It is not usually considered when discussing the four elements that are the foundation of Western zodiac.

THE THREE MODALITIES

Each horoscope possesses some combination of cardinal, fixed, and mutable qualities—unless one of these three modalities is absent. Each provides reliable layers of insight into the quality or makeup of a person's cosmic blueprint. Linked with activating forces, the dynamic *cardinal* signs are Aries, Capricorn, Libra, and Cancer. A central action associated with cardinal qualities is taking ordinary tasks to a new level and initiating action. The self-determined, willful, *fixed* signs are Leo, Taurus, Aquarius, and Scorpio. An important attribute of this modality is being bighearted with a keen sense of purpose. The *mutable* or changeable signs are Sagittarius, Virgo, Gemini, and Pisces. Their nature conveys strength and flexibility in mind, emotions, and spirit.

When one is looking at the wheel of the zodiac, these three modalities always move in the sequential counterclockwise order of cardinal (action), fixed (persistence), and mutable (flexibility). These three modalities are collectively called the triplicities. Their relations with the elements and Sun signs are as follows:

Element	Cardinal	Fixed	Mutable
Fire	Aries	Leo	Sagittarius
Earth	Capricorn	Taurus	Virgo
Air	Libra	Aquarius	Gemini
Water	Cancer	Scorpio	Pisces

What modality is connected with your sun sign? What is your personal experience of this energy? The following example is offered so you can see how someone might answer these questions: Let's imagine that you are a Scorpio, a fixed sign. Your mind is fixated or preoccupied with metaphysics, and you have an obsession with the Tarot and the runes. Once you learn that love for the occult is a noted Scorpio characteristic, your fascination with these oracles makes more sense, and you let yourself follow your dreams with greater passion.

THE PLANETS: EXPRESSIONS OF CONSCIOUSNESS

Each of the twelve sun signs is bonded with a planet that embodies an essential aspect of mind, body, emotions, and spirit. Because the planets move around the sun and sit in different constellations at different times, the qualities they personify take on varying degrees of meaning depending on their location in the sky.

The seven ancient planets used in astrology are Mercury, Venus, Mars, Jupiter, and Saturn, along with the sun and the moon. Even though the sun and moon are orbs, not planets, these great luminaries are treated as such by astrologers. The three outer planets, called transcendental or generational planets, are Uranus (sometimes called Herschel), Neptune, and Pluto. In Western astrology these three most recently discovered planets are included as corulers to three sun signs. The following list offers an introduction to some planetary qualities and their potential sway.

The Seven Ancient Planets

Sun

Planetary glyph: The circle equals spirit, wholeness, and completion. The dot in its center denotes spirit manifesting in matter.

Rules: Leo, the Lion

Gem: Ruby

Strength: Solar-positive yang energy, power, leadership

Weakness: Domineering, egocentric, pride

Moon

Planetary glyph: The half-circle crescent is linked with the receptivity and the spiritual crown of awareness.

Rules: Cancer, the Crab

Gem: Pearl

Strength: Feminine energy, intuition, depth of emotion

Weakness: Overly emotional, insensitive, overly protective

Mercury

Planetary glyph: The crescent (receptivity) sits above the circle (spirit), as it rests on a cross of matter.

Corules: Gemini, the Twins; Virgo, the Virgin

Gem: Emerald

Strength: Cleverness, communication, analyzing, healing

Weakness: Anxious, cynical, restless

Venus

Planetary glyph: A circle, sign of spirit, sits over the cross of matter.

Corules: Taurus, the Bull; Libra, the Balance

Gem: Diamond

Strength: Love, harmonizing, beauty, sweetness

Weakness: indecisive, fickle, narcissistic

Mars

Planetary glyph: A circle (spirit) is connected to an arrow (focus)
Corules: Aries, the Ram; Scorpio, the Scorpion
Gem: Coral
Strength: Power, passion, competitive, strong willed
Weakness: Aggressive, confrontational, impulsive

♃ Jupiter

Planetary glyph: An eagle (the soul) soars above matter.
Corules: Pisces, the Fish; Sagittarius, the Archer
Gem: Yellow sapphire
Strength: Expansive, ambitious, intelligent, generous
Weakness: Insensitive, extravagance, forbearing

♄ Saturn

Planetary glyph: The cross (matter) over soul and scythe (time)
Corules: Capricorn, the Goat; Aquarius, the Water-bearer
Gem: Amethyst
Strength: Responsible, hardworking, punctual, integrity
Weakness: Judgmental, strict, restrictive

The Three Transcendental Planets

Uranus

Planetary glyph: An H spear (either H for Herschel, last name of astronomer who discover Uranus) or three-pointed spear, over a circle (spirit)
Corules: Aquarius, the Water Bearer
Gem: Carnelian
Strength: Individuality, rebellious, eccentric, progressive
Weakness: Radical, riotous, eccentric

Neptune

Planetary glyph: The trident (spear of Hindu god Shiva; Roman god of the sea, Neptune; or both) over the cross of matter

Corules: Pisces, the Fish

Gem: Cat's-eye

Strength: Dreamy, psychic, visionary, idealism

Weakness: Delusive, secretive, confusion

Pluto

Planetary glyph: Circle linked with wholeness, over crescent (receptivity), over the cross of matter

Corules: Scorpio, the Scorpion

Gem: Onyx

Strength: Rebirth, transformation, generational awareness

Weakness: Dark moods, spectral, obscure[1].

Many of the attributes that describe the nature of these celestial bodies are tied to stories, legends, and myths associated with the early deities who share their name. For instance, the planet Mercury, the smallest planet, is equal to the Roman god Mercury (in Latin, Mercurius), who was known in ancient Greece as Hermes and was hailed as the almighty Thoth in Egypt. He was famous as the wing-footed messenger who channeled the wisdom of the gods to humanity, and his reputed talents include speed of intellect, cleverness, insight, changeability, powerful communications, commerce, and the gift of healing. The only planet named after a feminine deity is Venus, linked with many goddesses of love, fertility, and pleasure, including the Greek Aphrodite and the Norse goddess Freyja.

Retrograde Motion

Planets are considered to be retrograde when they appear to move in reverse motion while being viewed from Earth. Unwaveringly, astronomers agree that planets do not move backward; it's only an optical illusion.

Even so, the appearance of backward motion changes a planet's qualities from harmonic to disharmonic and indicates a change of nature. Here's an example: A phrase frequently discussed in astrology is "Mercury retrograde." When Mercury, linked with communication, is retrograde, the strength of its intended message may be challenged, delayed, changed, misunderstood, or weakened in some way. One positive side of this motion is that it's a great time to get work done.

CHAPTER 2

WANDERING INTO THE TWELVE HOUSES

The Western symbol for the horoscope is a 360-degree circle divided by twelve lines. It looks like a wheel with twelve sections, which are called houses. Each house represents one of the sun signs and an important aspect of human existence. In relation to the calendar year, the houses revolve through the ever-changing cycles of spring, summer, fall, and winter.

In Western astrology there are multiple systems for determining the degrees in each of the twelve houses, including Equal, Koch, Placidus, Meridian, and other variations. Once you advance your study, you can research the different systems to determine which system will work best for you. Within these pages I use the Equal house system. Each house, starting with the cusp of Aries, has a 30-degree segment in the zodiac wheel. I like this system because it offers a foundation for creating zodiac card spreads, the "Wheel of Life" rune cast, and card and stone readings when they are superimposed over someone's horoscope. (More on these topics in Part 4, "Divination's Doorway.")

As you visually move counterclockwise around the wheel of the zodiac, you're proceeding through twelve equally sized houses and each of the different sun signs in consecutive order. The first house on this cosmic wheel is Aries, the second is Taurus, and Gemini reigns over the third house, and as you continue going counterclockwise around the circle, you'll arrive in Pisces, the last sign, which governs the twelfth house. The lines between the houses mark the cusp or separation between one sign and its house from the next.

The meanings attached to each of the twelve houses parallel the agreed-upon attributes of the sun sign that naturally sits in a house. For instance, the fourth house is governed by the sign Cancer. The qualities assigned to the fourth house correspond to the most-prominent attributes of this sign: the mother, nurturing, the family, home, and security. The following fifth house, the home of Leo the stargazing lion, is linked with the qualities of leadership, creativity, entertainment, and children. Becoming familiar with the qualities of each house is a must to perform chart analysis. The primary significance of each of the different houses is as follows:

Qualities of the Houses

House	Sign	House Concerns
1	Aries	One's self, appearances, personality
2	Taurus	Finances, possessions & ambitions
3	Gemini	Personal expression, communications
4	Cancer	Home, family, security, mother
5	Leo	Creativity, children, romance
6	Virgo	Work, service, health, diet
7	Libra	Partnerships, marriage, commitments
8	Scorpio	Occult, taxes, death, others' money
9	Sagittarius	Philosophy, higher education, travel
10	Capricorn	Career, reputation, aspirations
11	Aquarius	Community, friends, associations
12	Pisces	The subconscious, dreams, secrets

WHAT YOU MIGHT FIND IN A HOUSE

Natural alignment of signs and houses of the zodiac

The first house sits on the eastern side of the wheel of the zodiac, where the sun's light awakens the morning's dawn. When you are looking at your horoscope, the constellation from where the sun's light is rising indicates your rising sign (where the sun was rising on the day you were born). Compared with the initiating energy of the element of fire, it's linked with the birth of one's ego, self-image, and soul sense of identity. It also depicts qualities of your physical appearance and how others view your appearance.

The second house, linked with the earth, indicates how a person steps into the material world to provide for physical needs and acquire finances. The limelight moves from "the self" in the first house to second-house concerns involving motivation, goals, desires for success, and wealth. Here begins the journey to acquire shelter, food, clothing, money, and other tangible goods.

The third house is bonded with the element of air, one's neighborhood, friends, and associates, including brothers, sisters, aunts, and uncles. Its attributes are communication, public speaking, technology, ideas, writing, sharing, and short trips to expand one's personal world. Here the intellect is held in high esteem.

The fourth house, ruled by the element of water, relates to emotions, the home, and feelings of being rooted to security (or not). It illumines relations with your birth mother or any other woman with whom you connect as your want-to-be mom. It's also linked with comforts and the second half or latter stages of life's journey.

The fifth house is home to the element of fire, romance, creativity, fashion, pregnancy, children, entertainment, and events that make you smile. Compared with the Dionysian quest to enjoy the moment, it's the celestial home for heated passions and experiences involving forbidden fruit.

The sixth house refers to the element of earth, the body, diet, healing remedies, coworkers, responsibilities, caregiving, and service to others. Sitting beneath the horizontal line of the zodiac's descendant, it involves the practical necessity of putting things in order—such as income and financial outflow, overall health, and well-being.

The seventh house concerns the element of air, marriage, cohabitation, contracts, and commitments of the heart. Because love is the supporting beam in its foundation, one can become lost in their reflection of significant others and their needs. Even if one doesn't have a primary relationship, having planets in this house can indicate that the dynamics (or karma) involving important others will be a focus, for better or worse, richer or poorer.

The eighth house is associated with the element of water, the occult, death, secrets, regeneration, taxes, funerals, inheritances, and resources of deceased kin. The question "Have you written your will?" accompanies the intense energy that can be felt when looking at the vista from the eighth house. Sex is also associated with this house, along with taboos and possessiveness, especially when wrapped with jealous ribbons of passion.

The ninth house is home to the element of fire, long-distance goals, foreign travel, ideals, higher education, philosophy, lofty visions, religion, gurus, and spirituality. Meditation, yoga, and contemplation for mastery of the mind are connected with diving into the depths of its panoramic perspectives.

The tenth house is home to the earth element and a chart's midheaven, where the fulfillment of ambitions, status, reputation, accomplishments, professional contributions, financial attainment, and skillful talent is paramount. If you hope to climb the highest mountain, look at the rulership of this house to analyze whether your inner goat has what it needs to ascend the peaks of your dream's summit.

The eleventh house corresponds to the element of air, friends, community, social and group connections, and your general meet-and-greet approach with humanity. It is bonded with the merits or demerits experienced through values playing out within the collective ideals of one's social communities.

The twelfth house represents the element of water, the subconscious mind, dreams, the imagination, past-life experiences, and the invisible depths of the psyche. Sometimes compared to a sealed manhole cover that hides potent forces from view, it is also connected with hidden agendas, miscommunicated motives, secret enemies, deceptions, and confinements.

Elements and Houses

The twelve houses can be grouped into four elementary categories:

Houses of Fire (action/reaction): House 1—personal views, house 5—personal interests, and house 9—spiritual views

Houses of Earth (money matters): House 2—material ambitions, house 6—work and occupation, and house 10—career fulfillment and reputation

Houses of Air (ideas/relations): House 3—relatives and community, house 7—partners, and house 11—friends and organizations

Houses of Water (emotions/intuition): House 4—second half of life, house 8—death/rebirth, and house 12—subconscious undercurrents

Each house acts as a reference point for analyzing qualities connected to the planets and a person's specific concerns. Many consider the house where a planet sits and its ruling element to the most-important features of a chart's interpretation.

If you're a beginning astrologer first learning to analyze charts, you will find that many do not follow the "natural" Aries first-house order. This occurs because the sun rises in a different celestial location every morning. The date, time, and birth location, unique to each person, determine where the sun rises on the line of the horizon and the constellation that rules the first house. Each ruler of the subsequent houses continues in order going around the zodiac wheel, following after the sun sign ruler of the first house. For example, the sun was rising in the constellation Libra on the morning of my birth. Therefore, Libra is my rising sign and the ruler of my first house. My second house will be ruled by Scorpio, Sagittarius will govern my third house, and the signs continue to be placed in houses around the wheel in their consecutive order. When you go around the zodiac and arrive at my twelfth house, you will see it being ruled by Virgo.

House Polarities

While looking at a natal (birth) chart that comprises twelve 30-degree houses, look at any house and note its sun sign ruler. Then look 180 degrees directly across the circle. The sun sign ruling the house sitting directly across the chart is its polarity. The following is a guide to the signs and their house polarities:

Aries, first house—Libra, seventh house
The first set of polarities is between the cardinal signs Aries, ruler of the first house of the self, and Libra. This sign of the balance rules the seventh house and one's commitments with others.

Taurus, second house—Scorpio, eighth house
The next set of polarities involves the fixed signs Taurus, ruler of the second house and personal finances, and Scorpio, ruler of the eighth house and finances involving others.

Gemini, third house—Sagittarius, ninth house
Ruler of the third house, mutable Gemini, involves immediate communications with neighbors and brothers and sisters, and short-distance travels. In the ninth house sits its mutable opposite, Sagittarius, which reigns over lengthy communications and far-distant travel.

Cancer, fourth house—Capricorn, tenth house
The fourth house, connected with the mother and water emotions, is ruled by Cancer. It sits at the nadir, or lowest point on the chart. Directly opposite is the tenth house, which sits at the zenith, or top point of the chart. It is ruled by Capricorn, the practical, earthly sign of financial status and material success.

Leo, fifth house—Aquarius, eleventh house
The next polarity involves fixed signs. Most fiery, Leos enjoy being in the spotlight. Aquarius, the airy humanitarian, likes to shine its light on the welfare of others.

Virgo, sixth house—Pisces, twelfth house
The mutable sign Virgo occupies the sixth, earthly house of career and health. Opposite in the watery twelfth house, Pisces loves to dive the depths of the imagination and dreams.

House Qualities

The houses are also considered to be either angular, succedent, or cadent. Angular houses are the first house (Aries), fourth house (Cancer), seventh house (Libra), and tenth house (Capricorn). They mark the cardinal points on the chart and indicate activating influences affecting the personality, style, commitment, and intentions of your querent.

The houses following the angular houses are called succedent houses. They are governed by the fixed signs: Taurus, Leo, Scorpio, and Aquarius. Succedent houses reveal how a person uses his or her own energy, where it is directed, and the weight of worldly responsibility being shouldered.

Next are the cadent houses, connected with the mutable signs of Gemini, Virgo, Sagittarius, and Pisces. Just as cadence or cadent means rhythm and movement, the energy represented by these houses showcases a potent flow of energies and adventurous experiences that a person may encounter or seek to avoid.

CHAPTER 3

A CELESTIAL VIEW OF THE HOROSCOPE

Defining Lines

Learning the meanings associated with the lines that create your horoscope adds useful dimensions to chart interpretations. The ascendant-descendant line (the horizontal axis) is drawn horizontally through the middle of the zodiac circle and divides the chart into two equal halves. In addition to dividing the circle in half, it points to polarities such as daytime-nighttime, dawn-dusk, spring-fall, oneness-otherness, and objectivity-subjectivity.

The bottom half of this circle denotes the Northern Hemisphere and houses one through six. The cusp of the first house starts at 0 degrees Aries, where the sun rises on the eastern horizon and illuminates one's rising sign. If most planet activity is on the bottom half of the chart, a person may be more inward or domestic by nature, self-contained, and private. Such a person will focus on their internal reactions and spend greater time reflecting on the truth within.

The top half of the zodiac circle represents the Southern Hemisphere and houses seven through twelve. If a person's planets appear mostly on the top half of the circle, which starts at the cusp of the seventh house (0 degrees Libra), he or she may focus mostly on external events and relations with others and be socially outgoing. This upper half of the horoscope can be compared to a magnifying glass that offers multifaceted views of one's relations, joys, frustrations, and challenges with the outside world.

As your eye travels around the zodiac wheel, if planets are scattered more or less equally through the top and bottom halves, the person may often be a combination of extroverted and introverted, social and antisocial.

Another important line on the horoscope divides the chart in half vertically (the vertical axis). It separates the eastern (sunrise) side from the western (sunset) side. If most planetary activity sits on the eastern side of the chart, it indicates that a person is independent minded and likely to focus on integrating the inner and external self with activities to experience the full spectrum of the zodiac wheel. If most planets are sitting in the western sphere of a person's chart, he or she is likely to be someone who is conscious of his or her interdependence with others and strives to fulfill their social responsibilities and obligations with others. The pursuit of adventurous, worldly experiences is high on their priority list.

This vertical line marks the cusp of the fourth house (0 degrees Cancer), called the I.C. (the Imum Coeli) or nadir, the lowest point on the chart. It depicts a person's inner foundation, their private sense of self, and their security. It sits directly opposite the M.C. (the Medium Coeli) or the midheaven point, at the very top of the zodiac circle. The zenith, or the highest point on a chart, is where the light shines brightest on your public life. It offers clues to how someone may live out their ambitions, reach their goals, and find fulfillment.

When looking at the circle of the zodiac with only the horizontal and vertical lines drawn, you see a circle with four quadrants—like a circle with a cross in the center. Not surprisingly, the globe bisected by meridian lines is the astronomical symbol for the earth itself and offers a clue to the underlying significance of the four quadrants.

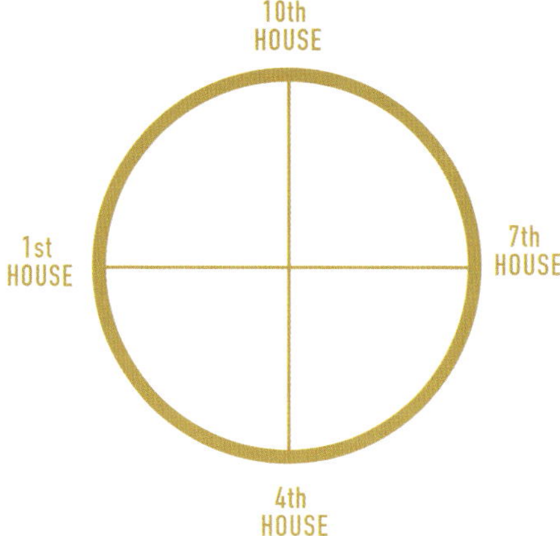

The horizontal line represents the horizon and marks the ascendant, between the first and twelfth houses, and descendant—the line between the sixth and seventh houses. The vertical line marks the nadir (the lowest point), between the third and fourth houses, and the chart's zenith (the chart's highest point), the ninth and tenth houses.

The first quadrant contains houses one, two, and three. Its significance is related to the self, or "Who am I?" concerns. The second quadrant holds houses four, five, and six. It's linked with our self-expressions, including artistic and occupational interests. The third quadrant contains the seventh, eighth, and ninth houses. It represents our relations and a growing awareness of our commitments and journeys with others. The fourth quadrant holds houses ten, eleven, and twelve. It is significant, with opportunities to fulfill our dreams, offer our capabilities to the world, and transform subconscious undercurrents into waves of conscious awareness.

FIVE MAJOR ASPECTS

Aspects are the relationships of one planet to another that are created by the angles formed by the number of degrees that exist between planets on the zodiac wheel. Mostly, there is a 6-to-10-degree allowable space between the exact degrees of the angles that are considered to be within the range for designating an aspect. The following descriptions introduce the five major aspects:

Conjunction—
Planets sit within 5 degrees of one another. Like two partners dancing the tango, their energies entangle with one another with a merged, get-up-and-go unified force. If the energies are harmonious or not depends on what planets are involved.

Oppositions—
Planets are 180 degrees apart. Sitting opposite from one another on the chart, they can be compared to being in a tug-of-war that can be either cooperative or fierce and challenging, depending on the planets involved.

Squares—
Planets are 90 degrees apart. This aspect is linked with confrontations, challenges, or obstacles that can ultimately bring a transformation.

Trines—
Planets sit 120 degrees apart. This "good energy" aspect is thought to be an expansive, harmonious blending of energies that can decrease conflicts.

Sextiles—
Planets sit 60 degrees apart. This aspect points to a flow of positive energies but is not as positive as the trine. It can indicate the development of potential, increased productivity, and having something to look forward to.

There are minor and unusual aspects, such as the semisextile, quincunx, grand cross, grand squares, and more. If your path takes you in the direction of becoming a professional astrologer, you'll need to become familiar with these and other aspects. With experience, you can become proficient in recognizing and discussing these planetary relationships.

LET YOUR CHART BE YOUR GUIDE

If you want to offer chart interpretations, you must be able to recognize zodiacal symbols. You will need to know the meanings associated with the sun signs, the planets, and the houses. Once you're confident of your understanding of these topics, you're ready to navigate around the wheel of the zodiac. Go from house to house and notice where the planets are placed. Also, if you plan on doing chart analysis, it's useful to have an **ephemeris** that lists the daily positions of the planets. It's an essential resource that lets you easily locate where the planets are in the sky at any moment in any given year, without depending on a computer.

When you first begin to read horoscopes, the easiest way to learn the many zodiac symbols is to have your birth chart available as your personal study guide. You can use it to explore the various chart components. It's the perfect starting point for an in-depth study. You can refer to your chart again and again as you learn about each item on it and gain insights about yourself while you're learning. It offers a never-ending opportunity to get to know your inner self through your unique celestial blueprint.

In the past, learning to create your horoscope used to be like learning advanced mathematics, but in current technological times the computer has made creating charts as easy as tapping a few keys. You can choose among widely available astrological programs that will ask you for birth date, time, and location of birth and then almost instantly crunch this information to construct your chart. Without needing to learn how to create a horoscope from scratch (unless you want to do this), you can obtain a chart and study its message.

If you need a chart, the appendix titled "Obtaining Your Horoscope" has a link to services where you can get your horoscope created online almost immediately, free of charge. If you don't already have your chart, now is the perfect time to have one created. Once you have a chart, the real work begins—decoding its messages.

Truly, you're deserving of a loving pat on the back for learning the content that is needed to be able to do chart analysis (please listen with your inner ear to the applause being sent your way). If it looks complicated at first, don't despair. If you take one step at a time, little by little you'll deepen your understanding of the attributes assigned to each of the signs, the planets, the elements, and the houses. If you start by finding your own "big three" on the chart—the sun, the moon, and the rising sign (determined by the sun sign ruler of your first house), you'll be walking through an entrance to a stargazing pathway connecting you with your inner self. It also provides insight into the luminous language of astrology.

When first viewing your chart, begin by looking at one house at a time. Examine their ruling sun sign and their accompanying attributes. Study the symbols for the planets and find the house where each planet sits. Think about the qualities attributed to each planet, and imagine a dialogue between a planet and the house where it sits. What do they each talk about? What are the benefits or detriments of a planet sitting in a house? How many of your planets sit in a house that is ruled by fire, air, water, or the earth element? What house tells you about your mother, father, siblings, lover, or enemies? Do you have any planets sitting in the houses relating to issues that are important to you?

Even if the study of astrology is a lifelong journey, you'll probably be surprised at how much you can learn in a short amount of time, while having fun with your practice. After you become comfortable talking about the planets and their meanings, location, and elements, it's time to advance to the next step: looking for and analyzing their major aspects, if there are any.

After you have a grasp on what's happening in your natal chart, you might enjoy trying an online search for "astrological charts of celebrities and famous people." If you do this and you're viewing a chart that is of interest to you, think about the attributes of the sun signs and the qualities of the different houses that they govern. What interpretations make sense to you when you look at their combined qualities? Think about how you can analyze the multiple planets connected with the qualities of the house where they sit. Once you can look at a chart and it makes sense to you, your analytical and intuitive processes will start developing into your unique approach to communicating the messages etched on the zodiac wheel. Don't push yourself to give readings if you aren't feeling ready. Each time you analyze a chart, you'll progress and become more knowledgeable.

As you understand how to discuss the components of the zodiac, not only will you be empowering yourself to be able to do chart interpretations, but you'll also be igniting the sacred fires of card and stone divination. Recognizing the symbolic components that create the wheel of the zodiac—specifically those that have been discussed in part 1, enables you to develop your ability to analyze the card spreads and rune casts being explored in part 4, "Divination Doorways." Once you turn the page, you'll begin the study of these two popular oracles.

> *Astrology is a diagnostic tool which has been given to Man so that he may begin to understand his roots in infinity and the higher laws of creation.*[1]
>
> —*Popular astrologer Alan Oken*

PART TWO

TWO PATHWAYS, ONE HIGHWAY

CHAPTER 4

MEETING THE CARDS AND THE RUNES

In olden times, the Norse were thankful for the gods who created them. They recognized their powers to keep the threatening frost giants at bay and to sustain the crops that fed their ravenous appetites. In return for such gifts, people worshiped their gods, the Aesir, who protected their hopes for tomorrow. However, it was the three Norns, the knowers of destiny, who intuitively knew if luck or misery ruled someone's fate. Whispering the secrets of the future among themselves, they would spin a thread of life for each and every person while watching destiny unfold from their home at the foot of the three-rooted world tree, Yggdrasil.

If only we had the ability of these three wise spirits to fathom the messages of the gods and to know the stories about the merits, demerits, and destiny of humanity. At least while we aspire to tap into the eternal voices that lay hidden in the evolutionary mists of time, we can work to hone our sensitivity to nonverbal messages, sharpen our perceptions, and stir the cauldron of our deeper knowing. We can humbly hope to be open to such possibilities and seek to understand the messages arising from the stars, cards, and stones.

When you begin to use these oracular mediums, you are embarking on an exciting journey. Learning to read their symbols can bring you face to face with the silent dialogues of both ancient and modern civilizations. Finding a road map to uncover the secrets of how to work with them requires combining the voice of your logic with the attentiveness of your intuition.

After you play and practice using these oracles, play with them again and again, and hold them near and dear to your heart, the insights needed to work with them will gradually be revealed—perhaps as if by magic! At times you might question why you, an intelligent person, are taking this unconventional path, but any uncertainties you experience will quickly disappear when you feel the wizardry of divinatory energies flowing through your being. For now, we begin by examining the Tarot and its significance, structure, and allure, and then we'll move forward to explore the vibrant palette of the runes.

ENTERING THE WORLD OF TAROT

For centuries the magnetic appeal of these seventy-eight playing cards has alerted humanity to the possibility of wisdom greater than the logic of conventional thought. Mostly used as a means to dive into the depths of the psyche, the Tarot is a timeless storybook reputed to illuminate truths hidden beneath the surface of conscious awareness. In modern times, the enchantment of its potency to unveil secrets is growing more popular every day.

The Tarot is an artistic rendition of the nature of existence, with detailed, symbolic portrayals. A storytelling game, it has twenty-two major and fifty-six minor cards. In this book, which connects Tarot with runes through the zodiac and their shared archetypes, the focus is solely on the twenty-two Major Arcana cards, known as trumps. Their images, pregnant with universal themes such as birth, transformation, and love, serve as keys to unlock the wisdom communicated through their nonverbal messages.

Its many symbols can be interpreted literally or metaphorically. They can be down-to-earth objects, such as an arrow pointing in a certain direction, or esoteric, such as a crown of royalty decorated with twelve stars that represent the twelve zodiac signs. When you play with the Tarot, you've adopted an excellent guide to teach you to communicate using the nonverbal language of symbols. Sometimes readers, including myself, choose to do readings using only the twenty-two trump or major cards. This practice is especially useful when doing short readings or when you're combining card readings with astrology or rune readings (or both). Since the twenty-two major cards are our focus in this text, if you have a deck, now is a good time to separate your major cards from the four minor suits. If new, your cards come that way. As long as it includes the Major Arcana, whatever deck you enjoy can be used to follow the various discussions and demonstration card spreads included in future pages.

If you don't yet know the meanings of all seventy-eight cards, learning to use only twenty-two is much faster than learning seventy-eight cards. When you start working with the majors, if you're willing, you can begin creating spreads that use only these cards. If you wait until you've also learned the significance of all fifty-six minor cards, you'll need to invest more time before you can start reading the cards (if you work with reversed cards, you need to become familiar with 156 interpretations). Additionally, if you become confident working with twenty-two major cards, there's a better chance you won't give up on learning the Tarot because of there being too many images to study. First learn to discuss the major cards, then learn the significance of the minor cards at your leisure. When you begin learning to interpret major cards, pay attention to their titles. The underlying meaning of each title, such as The Empress, Strength, and The Star, is rich with interpretive possibilities. As you read a card title, think about what it means to you, since it will provide clues to its interpretation.

Because these cards can be studied in relation to archetypes, mythology, the Kabbalah, the zodiac, alchemy, numerology, colors, the elements, facial directions and expressions, gender, philosophical content, sacred rites, and other potential classifications, there are various interpretations you can consider, depending on your personal views. Instead of worrying about how much there is to learn in order to read the cards, it's best to enjoy the journey. While viewing your cards, look for symbols that you recognize, and free-associate any ideas they might evoke in you. Free association is an internal process of thinking about one thing—for instance, a rabbit. Then, without controlling or criticizing where your mind goes, you watch the next idea arise in relation to it—perhaps fertility or Easter. Here's a Tarot example: Most cards titled The Hermit are illustrated with a flame in a lantern. In one person's mind after viewing this lantern, their thoughts go to their childhood camping trips. Because of this association, they view the flame as freedom from their norm. Another viewer might look at this flame and compare it to their religious beliefs, interpreting it as the Light of Christ or illumination on the path to awakening. All of these associations with the flame are personal and valid when discussing the Hermit's lantern.

Perhaps when viewing a card, you'll recognize a myth or story that relates to its image. Some images point to a card's astrological relationship. Any symbol you recognize can join your dialogue about the meaning of a card. For example, the first major card, The Magician, often shows a person wearing majestic robes. Over his (or, in some decks, her) head floats the infinity sign, indicating his cosmic nature. The Magician stands in front of a table decorated with four symbols that represent the four elemental energies: fire, earth, air, and water. Because of his charming appearance, you may view him as Merlin, the mythical wizard who possessed transcendent power in the legend of King Arthur. If you're a fan of Harry Potter, you might compare him with the magician Albus Dumbledore. As different as they are, both associations are valid and add meaning to this card's description.

The other fifty-six cards in the deck are called the Minor Arcana or lesser trump. They are equally divided among four suits. Each of the four suits has fourteen cards numbered from one to ten, and four court cards that traditionally depict noble royalty, starting with the page, then the knight, the queen, and, last, the king. Each suit represents one of the four elements, depicted as follows: wands equal the fire element (spirit), pentacles denote the earth element (body), swords stand for the air element (mind), and cups indicate the water element (emotions).

Although some modern deck creators may give other names to the major cards, their popular titles are as follows:

Number	Title	Number	Title
1:	The Magician	12:	The Hanged Man
2:	The High Priestess	13:	Death
3:	The Empress	14:	Temperance
4:	The Emperor	15:	The Devil
5:	The High Priest	16:	The Tower
6:	The Lovers	17:	The Star
7:	The Chariot	18:	The Moon
8:	Strength	19:	The Sun
9:	The Hermit	20:	Judgement
10:	The Wheel of Fortune	21:	The World
11:	Justice	0:	The Fool

Below is a chart showing some of the correspondences between the elements and the stars, cards, and stones:

The Four Elements and Esoteric Correspondences

Element	Astrology	Rune Spirits	Tarot
Fire	Spirit	Elves	Wands
Water	Emotions	Undines	Cups
Air	Mind	Sylphs	Swords
Earth	Body	Gnomes	Pentacles

Some deem the minor cards as less significant than the twenty-two major cards. However, every minor card points to the thoughts, feelings, or actions that might influence a person's choices. Each can widen the vista of a discussion's potentials, awaken the sleepy mind to new insights, and unveil the potential for earthly choices.

When viewing the cards, you'll see symbols that represent the natural forces and the influences of the four classical elements. When decoded, they offer clues to help you discover the messages within a card.

ORIGIN OF THE CARDS

There are different theories concerning the origin of the cards. The earliest traces of their history appear to be lost in the obscurity of time. Scholars note that a hand-painted deck of cards called Imperatori and the card game Tarocchi (designed by card lover Filippo Visconti, Duke of Milano) originated during the Italian Renaissance, sometime in the early 1400s. Its connection with royal nobility is visible in the court cards of this time, which were represented by kings, queens, knights, and pages. Others argue that they were already in existence as the nomadic Romani people brought them on their caravan trek from India to the European continent. Giving credence to this theory are the images in cards containing parallels to Indian mythology. For instance, the Hindu monkey god Hanuman has been portrayed carrying the images that represent the four Minor Arcana suits—the cup, wand, sword, and coin. The all-seeing eye of Shiva is comparable to the penetrating eye of the Egyptian falcon-headed god Horus, and searching behind the veil of illusion (Maya) to find truth.

Some teachers claim that the potent images were birthed in ancient Egypt, where they were used as prompts during sacred rites under the law of the goddess Hathor. Paul Foster Case, the founder of the Builders of the Adytum (B.O.T.A.) mystery school, profoundly states that

> the letters of TARO may be arranged to make the following five words: ROTA TARO ORAT TORA ATOR. "ATOR" is an old Latin form of the name of the Egyptian Goddess Hathor. . . . Thus this rather barbarous Latin sentence may be translated "The Wheel of Tarot speaks the Law of Hathor (the Law of Nature)."[1]

Also, because each major card corresponds to a letter in the Hebrew alphabet and can be correlated to the Tree of Life, a schematic map of the journey to enlightenment, some argue that the most probable origin of the cards is rooted in the Kabbalah. Still others believe that the cards surfaced in the lost continent of Atlantis to empower supernatural communications. Battles between good and evil, right and wrong, and darkness and light are constantly in play, with the world viewed as a playground for ever-unfolding dramas of dualities and dreams.

Whatever their origin, most will agree that it has been the fortune-tellers who are responsible for the Tarot's ongoing circulation, and that its potency for being used as an oracle began many centuries ago. In any case, unless an undisputed account of the Tarot's origins comes to light, its soulful teachings are frequently portrayed as an invitation to seek answers that exist far beyond the curious fascination of a fortune-telling card game.

Not limited to any one creed, the Tarot has an easy time fitting into most cultures and psychological systems. One who seriously invokes the relevance of its content and studies its symbolic language has an opportunity to partake in a nonverbal dialogue that is richly abundant with nondenominational, universal truths and eclectic, relevant wisdom. Self-discovery, transformative thinking, healing insights, and a heightened sense of belonging to a vast ocean of collective intelligence are some of the treasures it may offer.

GETTING YOUR CARDS

For many seekers, the initial inquiry is "Where can I buy a deck?" Luckily for most of us, we don't have to travel far to obtain cards. Access to the Tarot is as easy as a trip to the local metaphysical or online bookstore, where you can frequently find numerous decks with traditional as well as New Age designs. Although the mysteries of the Tarot may be veiled, hundreds of different new decks are appearing on the commercial market faster than readers can discover them. The deck that will work best for you typically depends on your Tarot experiences, personal interests, and design preferences.

If you're a beginning student, decks using common images are illustrated in a multitude of texts. You can read through a plethora of perspectives about the meanings of symbols and instructions on how to work with such decks. When you advance in your studies, occasions will likely arise when you have opportunity to play with innovative Tarot decks, and you may find some easier to read than others. As the saying goes, "Experience is the best teacher." This is certainly true when it comes to how most readers become adept at interpreting messages in a variety of visually unique decks.

When you start looking for a new deck, it's up to you to find one that screams out, "I'm yours!" Whatever deck you decide to call your own, you'll become more sensitive to its artistic language and the messages it communicates while playing with it.

Before buying your deck, if possible, go to a metaphysical or New Age shop or Schiffer's REDFeather Mind, Body, Spirit online shop, where you can look at copies of Tarot decks, do comparative shopping, and scan different cards. During your search, view the pictures of cards shown in books or featured on the web. When viewing images, do you like what you see? Do the card titles have subtitles that offer you guidance? You might prefer a deck that doesn't influence your interpretations with subtitles. If you have an opportunity to hold a deck, do you intuitively like how it feels? By finding a deck that feels perfect for you, your chances of wanting to play with it increase every time you shuffle. If you're not fond of a deck, you won't use it. If you have cards and stones that you enjoy holding, studying, and playing with, it will be easier to learn divination.

Some who are new in the Tarot community will ask whether a person must receive cards as a gift for them to work properly. Although sometimes readers can be happily surprised to be gifted a deck, this popular superstition isn't true.

Being a Tarot-card lover, I've never been able to patiently wait for someone to give me a deck when I want to experience a new one. When I buy a new deck, I take my time looking at designs, symbols, and the deck's overall theme, so I know I'll want to shuffle them. I hope that whatever cards you choose will work well for you, so you can experience a positive feeling while working with them. After obtaining your deck, if you're so inclined, wrap it in a beautiful cloth or keep it in a protective box. In doing so, you'll be honoring their sacred mysteries and also shielding them from becoming damaged. You can energize or charge them by letting them sit in the light of a full moon. This is also true when taking care of runestones as whatever oracle you are using. Honor the magical properties of your oracles by protecting them from worldly harm and treating them in a caring manner. Keeping them safe is a practical ritual that empowers your connection with them. Also, when your cards or runes are protectively wrapped, others won't easily reach for them. You have a choice whether to let others handle and play with them, or not. As much as I love my friends, I won't let them hold my oracles unless I'm giving them a reading. But I always keep my cards and stones nearby, even now when it's time to enter the enchanting realm of rune lore.

> Having fun playing with your cards and stones is your passport to a successful divination practice.

CHAPTER 5

CONNECTING WITH THE RUNES

The early cultures of northern Europe had a unique written language, distinct from the writing in any other region of the world. Composed of lined glyphs initially drawn on small pieces of bone, twigs, or stones, each unique symbol or rune conveyed its own noteworthy idea. Their meanings can still be found scattered in the stories, folklore, and legends of early Celtic, Germanic, Anglo-Saxon, Viking, and other northern European cultures. Commonly used to communicate with the gods, their enchanted messages were summoned to work magic, protect the weary, heal the broken, communicate the laws, and foretell coming events.

The word "rune" can be traced to its early usage, when it meant "secret," "whisper," or "mystery."[1] Beyond the comprehension of the masses, its mysterious, divinatory, and protective powers were woven into the rugged fiber of the various tribes of yesteryear's Nordic civilizations. Fast forward to current times, and the runes are used by many as an oracle in much the same way a person analyzes a chart or a reader views symbols on the cards. The glyphs are still used by those who wish to drink from the Well of Wyrd, a supernatural source of wisdom, to search for truths hidden within the rune's magical mysteries.

In the early history of the runes, instructions for invoking their powers were passed solely by word of mouth. Their cryptic messages were shielded from the untutored, who couldn't comprehend their significance. Those who demonstrated an instinctual ability to walk uncharted pathways into the unknown were called upon to channel divine messages and be the voice for the nonverbal communications told by the stones.

In early Nordic civilizations, when women milked goats and men herded oxen, most commoners didn't have access to a written language. Many would surely have been in awe of those rare souls who could read the runes and communicate with otherworldly powers. When life took a difficult turn, it was wise to seek the guiding perceptions of the honored ones who could converse with the spirits and speak on behalf of their ancestors. Many prophetic insights shined a ray of hope for easier times and guidance in how to be victorious over strife. Due to their soothsaying skills, the rune crafters were respected as keepers of magic, messengers of the Great Spirit, and the guardians of destiny. Sadly, if someone failed to give accurate predictions, they might be forced to dip into the murky bogs and face the chilling winds of an inauspicious fate.

THE ORIGIN OF THE RUNES

Just as the Tarot's origin is lost in shrouded legends of bygone times, so is the birth of the runes hidden behind closed curtains of antiquity. Believed to be prominent in 160 CE, these glyphs have been found scattered throughout northern Europe in the archeological remains of amulets, combs, metal shields, swords, scabbards, and stones. Slowly the runic glyphs evolved over a long period of watching how thoughts, words, and rituals aligned with various signs, symbols, stars, and seasons until they became a written discipline. However, it is Odin (Wodan), ruler of the Nordic pantheon, and god of magic, war, death, wisdom, and poetry, who is credited with their initial discovery and divinatory appeal.

The principal god of the Teutonic people, Odin could willfully change into any shape or size. On one occasion, he fearlessly embarked on a heroic journey of self-transformation to conjoin the nine realms of the Norse universe. Odin hung himself upside down for nine days and nights from Yggdrasil, the fabled tree of life, fasting without food or water. To accelerate his longed-for awakening and rejuvenation, he stabbed himself with his sword in a spirited rite of self-sacrifice.

This epic deed, described in *The Poetic Edda*, 1200 CE,[2] is compared by many to the portrait illustrating the Major Arcana card The Hanged Man. On the arduous last day of Odin's ritualistic journey, he looked at the ground beneath his hanging body and saw inscriptions written on little pieces of stone. With all the strength his weakened body could assert, he extended his arm downward and swept them into his hand. Instantly his powers heightened with an altered perception. Experiencing a thunderous sense of rebirth, he freed himself from the tree and shed the fragility of his old self. Understanding the unearthliness of the gift he had been awarded, he became empowered with a divine sense of responsibility for guarding the formidable energy alive within the runes.

The news of this miracle spread like a river of hope throughout this world and the "Otherworld," and the runestones became known as Odin's alphabet.

From the earliest of shadowed times, each deciphered message has been cloaked in muted sounds whispered throughout the lands where giants walked in the dark and clans could perish in war-ignited firestorms. Used by the mystic minded, runes could invoke the gods to petition for power, prosperity, protection, and peace. For the more worldly minded, they could also be used for practical matters, such as determining laws or discerning what deity should be called upon to escape an unfavorable fate.

In today's modern world, yesterday's bards and storytellers have been replaced with rune scholars, who probe the meanings attributed to each rune by delving into the poems, prose, legends, and myths of long ago. Many read *The Poetic Edda*, a collection of Norse verse, searching for the truth of the stones' significance, but their original concepts forever soar out of reach in the drifting sands of time. The hunt for bison and reindeer has been replaced with the pursuit of runic shards scattered in lingering embers of fiery battles long forgotten.

You might not be ready to cast a magical circle for a journey into runic astral dimensions, but if you're hoping to discover how to see with the eyes of a rune master, you might want to call on the spirit of Odin to guide you. Even if you don't want to rush to buy an amulet carved with protective runes, or have a love rune tattooed on your ring finger, consider taking a few moments to set a positive intention for having success working with these soulfully magnetic symbols.

THE RUNIC ALPHABET

In your studies you might come across Gothic, Icelandic, Welsh, Younger, and the popular Anglo-Saxon runic alphabet. The rune names listed below and throughout this text are the symbols found in the Germanic Elder Futhark, a twenty-four-letter alphabet. Its common form consists of three potent *aettir*, or family of letters. Each *aett* (the singular form of *aettir*) is divided into three groups of eight runes, and each group of eight is named after a widely acclaimed Norse deity. This practice was thought to invoke the powers of the gods or goddess and bring blessings to assist with matters concerning survival in human or Middle Earth realities.

The first aett is named honoring Freyja, goddess of love, nurturing, fertility, and beauty. It is associated with the fertile forces of creation such as cattle, being in tune with the rhythms of life and the power to succeed, and initiation into sacred realism. When the first letters in the first six runes are consecutively linked, it makes the word "Futhark."

Freyja's aettir

Elder Futhark Names	Common Names
Fehu	Feoh
Uruz	Ur
Thurisaz	Thorn
Ansur	Os
Raido	Rad
Kaunan	Cen
Gebo	Gyfu
Wunjo	Wynn

The second aett is led by Heimdall (you may read his name spelled Haegl, Hagall, Hoegl, or Hoel). This brave god of the rainbow was both a protector of the home and a powerful warrior who disrupted the complacent. The second aett is about the dangers on the battlefield of change, honor and respect, and the complexities and appreciation for life.

Heimdall's aettir

Elder Futhark Names	Common Names
Hagalaz	Hoegl
Naudiz	Nyd
Isaz	Is
Jera	Ger
Elhaz	Eoh
Perdhro	Peordh
Algiz	Eolh
Sowilo	Sigel

The third aett is named in honor of Tyr, also known as Teiwaz or Tiwaz. Famed for his courage, he was the fair-minded sky god of war, justice, legal action, swordsmanship, and communing with the sacred.

Tyr's aettir

Elder Futhark Names	Common Names
Tiwaz	Tyr
Berkanan	Beorc
Ehwaz	Eh
Mannaz	Mann
Laguz	Lagu
Ingwaz	Ing
Dagaz	Daeg
Opila	Ethel

When you read a variety of resources and different references, you'll find various spellings for the runes and their gods. For example, you may see the name of the god Odin as Woden, Odhin, or Voden. And you may see the last, twenty-fourth letter written as Daeg, Dagaz, Dueg, or Dag. The different spelling of names occurs because the runes were used at different times by various tribes in different regions in the northern world. The stories of their sacred markings were carried to separate territories and countries by merchants, hunters, warriors, and even prisoners. Each holder of the runes would interpret their names through their dialect, worldly time, and cultural view. Let your trusted resources help you determine the pronunciation of a stone's name. It can be a benefit to say each name out loud a multitude of times so you feel comfortable working with them.

ACQUIRING YOUR RUNES

Perhaps the search for your stones may feel like an impelling quest, an unexpected sway of alluring forces too strong to resist. Or, maybe you'll meet them in a museum or in your dreams through an enchanting mist beyond the world of certainty. In modern times, runes can be obtained in various ways. As with the Tarot, someone may give you a set or you can buy your own. If you're crafty, you can even create your own set.

If given a set of runestones that someone else has used, you'll want to do a cleansing ritual to clear the previous owner's vibrations. It's not that the stones will necessarily have bad vibes, but because you'll be drawing on your psychic senses to interpret their messages, it's important to clean them of others' imprints. You can compare doing a psychic cleansing to removing fingerprints from a glass window.

To cleanse your stones, you can let them sit uncovered where they can absorb the light of the full moon. Or, you can wrap your runes in a dark cloth and hide them within a secure box during a waxing phase of the moon. When performing a psychic-cleansing ritual, songs of gratitude or prayers for purification can reinforce your intimate bond. When chanting an invocation, call upon your inner bard to infuse them with blessed energy and imprint your heart's longing to hear their timeless voice.

If you're buying runes, feel their energy. If you do this simple, vibrational practice, you'll know if an oracle is right for you.

Besides conversing with other rune crafters to ask where you might find your stones, it's always fun to go to metaphysical shops, even online, and search for what's available. You might find sets created in ceramic, wood, quartz, crystal, or bone. At some shops, you can even find rune cards to shuffle or runic dice to toss. Before you make a choice, examine the stones to see that they're in good condition and the letters are clearly visible. As with Tarot cards, you'll be more willing to use them if you like the way they look and feel in your hand.

Check to see that they won't break easily if you accidentally drop them. If you can't examine them beforehand because you're purchasing from a mail-order supplier, ask your intuition, "Are these runes the right ones for me?"

Making Your Runestones

If you have an artistic inclination, you can make your own rune set. Your psyche will become their birthing channel, and you'll be united with them through an invisible umbilical cord to your subconscious.

Traditionally, runes were carved on tree branches or stones, but you can use any medium that works for you. When I was living next to the ocean, I painted my first set on small shells I collected during my morning walks on the beach. For my next set I asked a stonecutter to break a sheet of green jasper into twenty-four pieces. I then painted each piece with a silver rune letter. I chose the color green for my stones because I associate green with Mother Nature and healing. My glyphs were drawn with silver paint because this is a color I associate with intuitive energy. I drew the letters on my stones on a day with a full moon, hoping that this day would enhance my intuitive connection with them.

While initially learning to work with the runes, I practiced drawing the letters on 2-by-3-inch note papers. Because I'm not an artist, my glyphs looked like something a child would draw, but my hand-drawn runic letters helped me learn to recognize their shapes, titles, and key meanings.

When you're deciding on materials for creating your rune set, find and use materials and colors you enjoy. For example, if you associate the color red with anger, you might not want to use this color for your stones. On the other hand, if you associate this color with love and high energy, red stones will be perfect for your work, since you have a positive connection with this color.

When engraving or drawing your runes, be patient and work in a deliberate manner. Set aside time when you're not pressured by worldly demands or emotional stress. To help you focus on the potency of each mark, think about their meanings and etch their higher purpose into your mind.

If you take part in rituals, you might want to call upon the goddess Arianrhod, the Lady of the Moon, to weave her magic into a blessing to empower your stones and guide your work. Or you might call upon Lady Morgan, Celtic goddess of magic and divination, and ask her to help strengthen your communications with them. You might even be inspired to write songs about the stones, or to read poetry written by those whom the magic in runes has touched. Well-respected rune caster Thomas Michael Caldwell has authored such a poem on how one can call upon them to get through the difficulties of day-to-day modern challenges:

The Ancient Runes

by Thomas Michael Caldwell

In times of much complexity
When nothing seems aright
On darkest days, we search within
To seek a source of light

We look for guidance, in the past
And reminisce the good
Remember how our people lived
And deep inside, still would

We come from a Folk of Magick
When myth and life were one
We worshiped gods of ancient kin
Beneath the midnight sun

Our father's fathers told their tales
By shade of trees they schooled
Upon the Earth, alive and green
Of how the gods once ruled

A treasure trove of value great
For mortal man below
An arsenal of weaponry
To fight the pain and woe

The Allfather was one of them
Who loved his children dear
He gave an eye for wisdom's sake
And did so without fear

He hung alone for nine long days
And nine long nights in all
An alphabet that came from blood
And through the Ages call

Accept the gift he's given you
And over many moons
Use for wisdom, power, and good
The ancient, sacred runes

CONNECTIONS AMONG THE CARDS AND STONES

Some poetry showcases the beauty of Tarot and astrology as well as the runes. We're so lucky to have these possibilities included within the play box of our imagination. When studying these oracles, trust your insights to discover their secrets and let your heart listen to what they want to tell you. Once you have a sense of one card's or stone's meaning, look to the stars and find their astrological connections to acquire a celestial pathway to delve into their significance.

As stated earlier, these oracles share a primary partnership through parallel correlations on the zodiac wheel. Each rune has a counterpart with a major Tarot card and a sun sign or planet. Once you become aware of their astrological correlations, you have specific information that points to the comparability of their interpretations. Utilize their shared celestial and archetypal themes to open the gateway for viewing a kaleidoscopic synthesis of their significance.

To encourage you to find connecting points among the stars, cards, and stones, the following two exercises are offered. The only rule for you to follow is to have fun. As much as you can, follow the guidelines (or create your own) to help you become acquainted with their interconnections.

A Daily Exercise

Take one Tarot card from your deck. Find its astrological association. Next, look up the rune that matches the same astrological correspondence. Take this rune from its pouch. Next, place this stone and Tarot card near one another, face up on a table. Now find a piece of paper and draw their matching zodiac symbol on the paper and place it near them. For at least two or three days, as you walk by or sit at the table where these three images are placed, glance at them without any demanding effort. When you have a few extra moments, have a "meet and greet" exchange with them. Dialogue with them as if they're your new best friends. Silently ask them about their benefits or detriments, their purpose, and any questions you have in relation to their importance. How do they answer questions that you ask them? Search for clues about their meaning that can inform you about their energies. Concentrate and meditate on their names, titles, colors, forms, symbols, and celestial unity. Examine your personal understanding of how they speak to your heart. Can you easily discuss your emotions with them? After you feel a kinship with their essence, inwardly ask a meaningful question about your life. Allow each of the three connected images to answer your question. How do they each enlighten your self-inquiry and inner knowing?

Once you feel well acquainted with these three associated images, it's time to put them away. Now it's time to bring the next trio of corresponding imagery to your table and start your next exploration of themes, meanings, and associations with them. As you did with the previous group of three images, silently dialogue with them, enjoy getting to know them, and ask them their meanings. Let them answer a question that you have about yourself. Have fun with your celestial conversations. In a short amount of time, with consistent practice, you'll develop an understanding of the significance of the major cards and runes in relation to their zodiac connections.

Having intimate conversations with your oracular mediums enables you to become familiar with their themes and celestial connections. The following guide is offered as a template to help you organize, analyze, and record your studies.

Template

Insights into the Stars, Cards, and Stones

Date and time:

___

The name of the sun sign or planet to be discussed is

___

Draw its symbol here:

What does this symbol mean to you?

___

___

___

What Major Arcana card is associated with this astrological image? What do you see in this card?

___

___

___

What runestone is linked with this celestial image? What does it represent to you?

___

___

___

What imaginings do you have about each of the three images? What feelings, ideas, or associations are triggered when you look at them?

___

___

___

Do you see any common qualities in this divinatory trio? What astrological connections do they share?

Such discussions concerning the stars, cards, and stones can be used to resolve their mysteries and clarify their interpretations. As you become more experienced discussing your oracles, many questions that you have about them will be answered through ongoing practice. Your inclination to light the lamp of oracular wisdom offers a deeply personal understanding of how to weave a colorful story with their connectedness.

Once you commit to taking this sacred journey, it's your willingness to practice that will accelerate your success. At this juncture, the key words are *shuffle your cards* and *toss your stones*. If you're asking how to shuffle cards and toss your runes, please read the instructions in part 4's introduction.

When you're ready to view the correlations and their discussions, it's time to turn to part 3, "The Mystical Library," starting with chapter 6, "Gazing through an Astrological Lens."

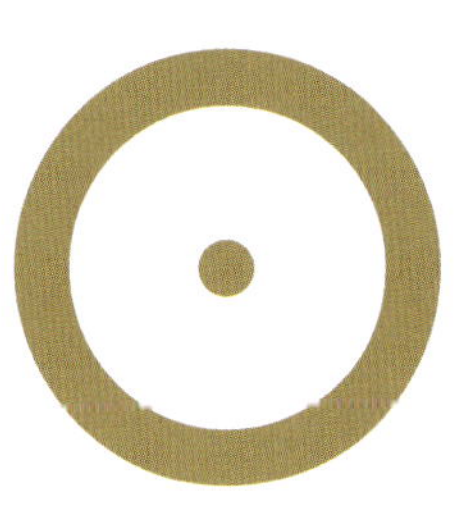

Consider what these symbols mean to you: The Sun, The Sun card, and the rune Gyfu.

PART THREE

THE MYSTICAL LIBRARY

CHAPTER 6

GAZING THROUGH AN ASTROLOGICAL LENS

Newsworthy Notes

To walk the path of a seer requires passion, a willingness to hear the flutter of angel wings, and a mind filled with the courage to walk through both visible and invisible corridors to balance the known with the unknown. Since you've arrived at this gateway, you must possess some of these qualities, or maybe all.

Your knowledge of basic astrology, its keywords, and its archetypes are like superfoods that will increase your potency to discuss the oracles. As you enter the Mystical Library, this introduction provides some insights to support your exploration.

The Infinite Worth of Every Keyword

A gift of current times is that everyone is blessed with a gourmet menu of choices for exploring the worlds of astrology and oracles and the realm of divination. You can study signs, symbols, archetypes, alchemy, psychic development, numerology, mythology, and various courses on how to dive into the oceanic waves of the subconscious to search for undiscovered truths. Because you can spend your entire life questioning the messages whispered by a source beyond knowing, it's a benefit to seek a means to expand your access into your third-eye vistas.

Although there is never a single formula for learning how to divine, the key qualities discussed at the end of each astrological, card, and rune description point to their universal themes and a palette of concepts that can increase your understandings of their meanings. You will see that the universal qualities presented at the end of each description can be shared equally among the three mystical arts. You can use these comparisons as a resource to help you become acquainted with their interconnectedness and learn their unified, common archetypal themes and shared qualities. You don't have to memorize these key attributes, because when you view the cards and the stones through the window of astrology and their shared archetypes, you'll begin to ignite your sixth sense about how these oracles have some comparable symbolic components.

If you've already been studying these divinatory arts, you might have adopted your own keywords or phrases for the various symbols. You can incorporate your own ideas as companions to the keywords and qualities described here. Be flexible to finding ways to juggle diverse ideas and expand the dimensions of your work in whatever ways lead toward your success.

Psychic Development 101: Voice Your Ideas

Both studying other people's interpretations for oracular images and learning the meaning of symbols through your personal associations have their value. Whatever path you follow to learn their meanings, your intuition will magically grow when you call on it repeatedly to guide your interpretations. Instead of striving to memorize the multitude of meanings for each planet, or upright or reversed card, or straight-up, sideways, or downturned stone, you might simply ask, "What does this star, card, or stone mean to me?" With the evolution of your study and practice, you'll learn from experience how to identify the most-important themes for your discussions.

Also, analysis of the time-honored meanings connected with the stars, major cards, and stones will help you develop a solid foundation for creating interpretations. Such well-earned information can help you build a reliable structure for your reading's narratives. You can also let the key qualities and archetypes that you will meet in the following pages serve as springboards to help you grasp their significance. When working as a reader, as long as your heart is open to the images drifting through your perceptions, interpretations will come into your sixth sense like a leaf falling in the wind.

> Interpreting the astrological, Tarot, and rune symbols will help you learn to listen to your intuition.

Universal Imagery: The Archetypes

When you explore archetypes, you're setting out on an adventure into the core of your awareness, where you can meet the collective unconscious. It extends into the limitless mind of creation, where you can touch the oneness within existence.

The archetype is one of Carl Jung's central concepts. It refers to an experience or universal mental pattern that's expressed in a person's way of experiencing the world. "Universal" means that it's something that exists among all people everywhere in one way or another. Archetypes contain qualities, patterns, or aspects of ourselves that all of humanity can identify with—at least to some degree.[1]

As my coauthor and I wrote in *Tarot at a Crossroads*, archetypes are "timeless beyond language and race, for the most part they live free from the doctrines of culture, place, and traditions."[2] As universal patterns, they stand in contrast to that which is individual and unique. Archetypes can be recognized in our ordinary reality, our dreams, and our myths and fairy tales. A few examples are the hero, the healer, the hermit, and the Grim Reaper, but their list is extensive.

If you're looking at life in 200 CE in cold, northern cultures, you may not know much about the practical day-to-day living, such as what kind of plumbing people might have had, but all will agree that everyone had a father, and that his essential roles must have been similar in many ways to today's modern dads.

Also, when you look at the father as an archetype, you might recognize additional archetypes that he personifies. You may see him as the wise old man, the rescuer, the rebel, or even the magician. Or, you might even consider him to be the stereotypical archetypal authoritarian. Each association can include qualities that timelessly recur in the woven inner tapestry of collective humanity.

Why should the different archetypes matter to you? Because understanding them enables you to have a more penetrating insight into human nature and a view of what's going on in its infinite depths. Like recurring dreams, when you recognize their common patterns, it can help you understand the role they assume in the psyche. It can also help you decode the universal messages in the zodiac, the Tarot, and the runestones. When reading my following interpretations, if you determine that an image has a different archetype than the one I suggest, it's best to follow your own insights. The truth is that most likely we're both right, though we're each right for different reasons.

A RENDEZVOUS WITH THE TWELVE SUN SIGNS

Use the various interpretations that follow to help you brainstorm ideas to increase your understanding of how to read the oracles. With a little help from your oracular muses, and your willingness to practice, your success will come. It's your ongoing work with these mediums that will help you build the skills you need to divine.

You will see that keywords listed in this library have examples divided between the self and the shadow. The self represents qualities connected with a positive sense of being and becoming. The keywords aligned with the shadow indicate areas that may be challenging, and the work needing to be done to maintain balance. As your understanding of symbols and their potential interpretations grow, you'll find that the boundaries to their specific meanings will also expand.

The following discussions are offered to help you build a divinatory foundation. At this juncture the keywords are "courage," "confidence," and "exploration."

Aries, the Ram

Boldly leading the way for other sun signs to follow, Aries sits at the helm of the first house. The first sign on the natural zodiacal wheel, Aries rules the dawning of spring, the budding of life, surging energy, fertility, and the germination of original ideas. Its time begins with the vernal equinox around March 21, when the tilling of the earth softens the cold soil and dormant seeds sprout anew. What has been hidden in the darkness of the Northern Hemisphere's winter receives the sun's invitation to awaken.

Ruled by the planet Mars, Aries has ties with the Roman god of war who shares its name. In ancient Greece, the god Mars was prayed to as Ares, who was glorified with unmasked courage and a fiery, competitive nature. Many myths and legends weave tales of valor, glorifying his fierceness and willingness to lead others in battle.

Although associated with the aggressive warrior who's willing to combat others face to face, not all Aries are fighters. Even those who appear charged for battle can turn their fierceness into peacemaking efforts when called upon to resolve sensitive issues. When celebrating intimacy, the tenderhearted desire of the Aries to be loved can turn their passion sizzling hot. Whether a lover, leader, follower, or fighter, this sign symbolizes high energy, potency, and the uncanny willingness to blaze a trail where others fear to tread. If they appear to lack patience, it's because their inner diligence is standing alert, waiting for a signal to take action. But, when hooked into a stubborn stance, it can be to their benefit to seek others who may moderate their view.

Connected with the Emperor card and the rune Tyr, the archetypal Aries are strong-minded, independent thinkers. Seldom liking to be told what to do, they're natural leaders who tend to act as quickly as fire jumps through dry brush. However, these zodiac initiators enjoy listening to the perspectives of others and can usually be counted on to do good for the world.

Keywords for Aries

The Self
Daring, proactive, takes initiative, original thinker, pioneering spirit, potent, determined, independent, athletic, courageous

The Shadow
Self-absorbed, inflexible, aggressive, hot tempered, provocative, bossy, intolerant

Stirring the Mystic Cauldron

When Divining, These Align with Aries
The card: The Emperor
The rune: Tyr
The archetype: The leader

Qualities They Share
Strong will, ambition, courage, independence

Taurus, the Bull

The bull, a powerful animal with massive horns, was considered sacred in olden times. Once idolized for its fertility and potency, Taurus, a Venus-ruled sign, is associated with the solidity of the earth element, fruitfulness, financial know-how, and practical power. Its zodiac nature is linked with the archetypal shaman, who has the wisdom to fearlessly enter both the supernatural and the material realms, and the know-how to grow flowers of prosperity even in parched soil.

Although the bull is a sign of prosperity, riding one is dangerous, as can be testified by Princess Europa, who attracted the lustful attention of the ultimate shaman, the Greek god Zeus. Shape-shifting into the form of a mighty bull, Zeus enticed her onto his back, then jumped into the Phoenician waters and carried the maiden across the sea to Crete. He then morphed into the form of a playful raven and seduced her before shifting back into his humanlike body and making her the mother of three of his sons.

The power to plant seeds of love is assigned to Taurus, adding to this sign's reputation of having a nurturing heart under a forceful and sturdy determination. But even when roses of success are blooming, the energetic natives of this sign will still spend long hours tilling the soil of their mighty ambitions. If they must travel for either business or romance, communications are spoken with a commanding voice with the hopes of securing solid ground beneath their efforts.

Associated with the High Priest card, and the rune Ur, both share the attributes of power, potency, and endurance. Beneficially linked with primal instincts, those represented by these signs know when to chase rainbows and when to seek protection from the storms. As long as one doesn't get lost searching for daisies in winter's frozen fields, and he or she keeps charging forward, their hard work generally ensures tangible results and successful efforts.

Keywords for Taurus

The Self

Forceful, determined, potent energy, down-to-earth practicality, lover of truth, stable, affectionate, materialistic, spiritually minded

The Shadow

Bullheaded, breaks down fences, demanding, compulsive, overly sensitive, impractical financially, lacks flexibility

Stirring the Mystic Cauldron

When Divining, These Align with Taurus

The card: The High Priest
The rune: Ur
The archetype: The shaman

Qualities They Share

Determination, fertility, stability, affection

Gemini, the Twins

Gemini, the sign of the twins born from a cosmic egg, is characterized as quick witted, intellectually sharp, and acutely aware of the need for better communications in the world. A Mercury-ruled sign, it is linked with the Greek god Hermes, the scribe for the gods who became Mercury in Rome, noted for winged sandals that helped him move quickly between the divine and mortal worlds, and the Egyptian equivalent Thoth, known for inventive and magical skills.

Geminis are said to have inquiring minds, clever ideas, farsightedness, and energetic spirits. Curious, they enjoy travel and expanding their realm of existence while viewing polarities such as light and darkness being reflected both in movement and the stillness. Their journeys may include adventures in the world of science and lofty thinking while they surf the up-and-down, positive and negative waves of life. Bright and young spirited, the Gemini archetype, the messenger, is shared with the Lovers card and the rune Eh. Versatile in thought, word, and actions, these personalities will relentlessly seek ideas that penetrate deep into the "how" and "why" of life. With acute understanding of emotional complexities, they can relate to a wide range of different life choices and be sympathetic both to the pros and cons of any argument, even when controversial. Known to be restless, Geminis are usually eager to move ahead and pursue their interests with haste.

With the wind that blows the airy Gemini's ideals sky high comes the cross currents of noble ideas to activate communications for the greater good. Even looming storm clouds on the horizon of duality can't stop them from holding tight to their dreams. Frequently successful, striving to fulfill one's highest potential is a natural trait.

Keywords for Gemini

The Self
Clever, mentally versatile, inventive, travel minded, perceptive, penetrating, quick witted, communicative, the networker of ideas

The Shadow
Opinionated, overly verbose, changeable without notice, logic blocks intuition, impatience, restless

When Divining, These Align with Gemini
The card: The Lovers
The rune: Eh
The archetype: The messenger

Qualities They Share
Unity, communicating, choices, duality

Cancer, the Crab

Never too tired to count the countless stars, Cancer, the archetypal nurturer, is connected with the mother, the feminine psyche, emotional depths, nest building, imagination, intuition, and the domestic and esoteric arts. Its ruler, the moon, has a gravitational influence on the rhythmic flow of ocean tides that energizes the up-and-down waves of change. With a strong lunar bond, the Cancerian watery ability to surf the emotional undercurrents of others surges through feelings with a reflective, knowing sway. Often accompanied by an alluring smile, beneficial insights, and a hearty hug, they will dive the depths to resolve issues swirling in subconscious memories.

Open to flowing with the alternating and sometimes surprising currents in the River of Life, the archetypal Cancerian, linked with the rune Eolh and the Chariot card, is deeply sensitive—sometimes more so than they want others to know. Just as the crab likes to retreat into its shell and hide in the sand, they are known to bury their complex feelings and make convincing excuses to avoid confrontational exchanges. But they don't need to worry, since the Greek moon goddess, Selene (also known as Luna), who successfully steered her sun-reflecting chariot through the heavens and back again within a lunar month, is their celestial guardian.

Although organizing cupboards and cleaning the house might not be a favorite task, this sun sign's personality is a natural homebody. Even while intense feelings may be pounding in their hearts, they are known to fiercely protect those they love and work unselfishly to help sustain Mother Nature and benefit those whom they hold close.

Keywords for Cancer

The Self
Openhearted, strongly emotional, sensitive, receptive, imaginative, domestic, maternal, protective, nurturing, sympathetic, intuitive

The Shadow
Overly sensitive, moody, critically analyzes emotions, insecure, worries too much about others, gets lost in memories

Stirring the Mystic Cauldron

When Divining, These Align with Cancer
The card: The Chariot
The rune: Eolh
The archetype: The nurturer

Qualities They Share
Receptivity, protection, change, clairvoyance

Leo, the Lion

Leo, the royalty of the stars, is governed by the sun, the bestower of light, brilliance, and life-giving forces of nature. Known to be self-determined, positive minded, and creative, those born beneath the sign of Leo are not shy about expressing their zeal for life. When they fine-tune their focus and direct their talents toward leadership, they can tap into their outgoing disposition and boldly spring to the front of most crowds.

A fixed fire sign personality, Leos are known to frequently dazzle with the sparkling energy of the archetypal enchanter. Like the Egyptian sun god, Ra, believed to provide the light of day, when empowered, a Leo can illuminate the darkness, seduce others with charisma, and step into a center-stage role.

You'll also meet this archetype when viewing the Strength card and the rune Cen, both reputed to call upon the might of a lion when leaping toward their goals. Bravely in love with life, they have a natural instinct to find golden opportunities and seldom stray far from their pride (group of lions). One way or another, they're good at finding what they need when it's really important to do so, even when it involves transforming the mundane into the mystically enchanting.

In accord with the saying "No sign is perfect," when the regal nature of the Leo becomes too power hungry, they can fall from whatever high branch they've climbed. When this happens, their normal warmth can turn into an offsetting chill. But since the wisdom of the Leo is commonly heart centered, they're usually inspired to make peace with the world. Quick to forget and forgive, they embrace the wisdom of love and selflessly offer their healing warmth to those in need.

Keywords for Leo

The Self
Prosperity, solar-positive energy, fiery will, enthusiasm, entertaining, outgoing, affectionate, courageous, creativity

The Shadow
Egotistic, overconfident, self-centered, dominating, seeking center-stage attention, fearful of rejection

Stirring the Mystic Cauldron

When Divining, These Align with Leo
The card: Strength
The rune: Cen
The archetype: The enchanter

Qualities They Share
Vitality, boldness, heroism, happiness

Virgo, the Virgin

Mercury, the planet associated with communication, quickness of thought, critical perceptions, intellectuality, and persuasiveness, rules over Virgo, the mindful perfectionist. Their strong mental qualities combine with the practical, steadfast influence of its element, earth, to inspire structure, solidity, and fertility in relation to achieving goals and success. With an innate ability to analyze and discriminate, they are unusually good at making decisions, prompting some to combine this sign with the thinker and the insightful sage archetype.

Virgo is symbolized by the Virgin, steadfast in her efforts to harvest wheat. Similar to the Tarot's Hermit card and the runestone Ger, this sign's starring reputation as being sharp witted can sometimes be dimmed by their critical-mindedness. Naturally curious and open to new ideas, Virgos seek to understand the higher meaning of serving others, especially in domains related to health and career. Often a merciless workaholic, a Virgo's instinctual know-how longs to realize a greater mission, fulfill material goals, and seek just rewards, such as a well-deserved pay raise.

With a tendency to organize, plan, and cultivate the soil of prosperity, Virgos never tire of fulfilling commitments and making their talents shine. When facing challenges, they'll shift mental gears and speed their ways to safe ground. Some seek to reap the supreme harvest of spiritual enlightenment, while others silently probe their soul calling and a visible means to turn on the Light of Material Prosperity.

Keywords for Virgo

The Self
Mindful, analytical, scholarly, systematic, perfecting, organizing, hardworking, connecting with healing energy, career focus

The Shadow
Worrisome, nervous, overly methodical, faultfinding, self-critical, distracted by stress, needing to improve diet or health (or both)

Stirring the Mystic Cauldron

When Divining, These Align with Virgo
The card: The Hermit
The rune: Ger
The archetype: The sage

Qualities They Share
Analyzing, finances, healing, wisdom

Libra, the Scales of Justice

Sign of the impartial scales of Lady Justice, Libra is ruled by Venus, associated with romance, pleasure, beauty, poetry, music, drama, and the arts. They're deeply aligned with fine-tuning the voice of love, and it's hard to imagine Librans being blindfolded and holding a two-sided, sharp-pointed sword of judgment, indifferently weighing the merits of the good and bad, truth and lies, and the pleasing and the painful. It's much easier to envision this sign's archetype, the diplomat, linked with the card Justice and the rune Gyfu, living with a smile on his or her face while searching for balance and social harmony. Extroverted by nature, they are typified as having attractive, friendly, and caring personalities with a keen sense of knowing how to open closed doors to partnerships, parties, and intimate involvement.

Although Libras are usually peacemakers at heart, it doesn't stop them from being vulnerable to misleading claims and emotional manipulation. On their good days, even when dealing with complications, they are reputed to be tactful and willing to be more than compromising in order to meet in the middle. Because Libras tend to balance both the pros and cons of every story, they resist making up their minds, leaving judgments about others to dangle indefinitely out of reach.

Only the stars know how this judicious diplomat and unsurpassed mediator can also have a reputation of being like a fish out of water when making decisions. Yet, maybe it's because they tend to make choices to climb mountain peaks of positive possibilities that they don't want to juggle and judge choices that take time away from their preferred pursuits. Even if they're sometimes hopelessly indecisive, soulful communications, light, and love are the master lyrics heard in the songs they sing.

Keywords for Libra

The Self

Loving, friendly, sociable, tactful, fair-minded, cooperative in partnerships, harmonious, charming, artistic, mediating

The Shadow

Insecurity, indecisive, yielding, gullible, easily infatuated, love-crazy, imbalance, can be manipulated by other's emotional needs

Stirring the Mystic Cauldron

When Divining, These Align with Libra

The card: Justice
The rune: Gyfu
The archetype: The diplomat

Qualities They Share

Balance, collaboration, fairness, mediating

Scorpio, the Scorpion

Scorpio, jointly ruled by Mars and Pluto, is connected with physical action, willfulness, the potential to change, transformation, inevitable death, rebirth, and the occult. Some people would rather forget that this sign can point to the possibility of physical death, and prefer to link it with high sexual energy, renewal, and regeneration. Bonded to the archetypal phoenix rising from the flames, it embodies the steady evolution of the psyche and its transformational potency.

Scorpios are sometimes characterized in relation to their sign, the scorpion, and its means to deliver a revengeful sting. Other negative qualities can include resistance to change, jealousy, and possessiveness, but usually their high Mars energy keeps them moving faster than anyone who might point the finger at such behavior. With the penetrating eyes of an eagle and their seductive smiles, they are known to be passionate, intensely emotional, intuitive, and magnetically attractive.

Some Scorpio personalities can get lost in their mind while looking away from the world and waiting for a signal to fertilize transformational seeds of the Tree of Life. Or, they can be driven by their understanding that the otherworldly Tree of Death, planted by the Greek god and king of the underworld, Hades, is sprouting vines around their finite time. Because the card Death and the rune Eoh correspond to this sign, their watery yet sometimes hot and steamy attributes, such as Scorpio's secretive nature, can be challenged by a Stoic dam of private emotions. When the potential for change draws near, their intuitive sense shifts into high gear to navigate unpredictable currents and ensure alignment with their soul sense of purpose.

Keywords for Scorpio

The Self

Strongly emotional, sensual, instinctual, willful, resourceful, penetrating, secretive, past-life visions, potential for change

The Shadow

Possessiveness, jealousy, mood swings, emotional complexity, overly protective, unforgiving, a flood of anger

When Divining, These Align with Scorpio
The card: Death
The rune: Eoh
The archetype: The phoenix

Qualities They Share
Secretive, rebirth, transformation, the psychic

Sagittarius, the Archer

Symbolized by the centaur, a seductive creature with a head and torso of a man combined with a muscular body of a horse, the Sagittarius holds the arrow steady with mindful awareness and singularly pointed concentration. Comparable to the might of this mythical beast, these willful archers know how to focus and aim the aspiring mind toward lofty targets of their energetic ambitions. Intellectually bright and turned on to cosmic ideas that show how to make the world a better place, these fiery folk don't mind walking the extra mile to overcome limiting boundaries. They seldom waste time and work with an unmatched intensity to manifest their dreams of fulfillment for living a successful life.

With Jupiter— planet of expansion, optimism, the guru, and higher education—being this sign's ruler, their ambitions can include satisfying more than their own needs. True idealists who consciously strive to share their hard-earned wisdom, they are happy to shoot their mental energy toward helping the world evolve in the direction of its greater good.

Because Sagittarians embody the spirit of philosophical understanding and spiritual guidance, their sign is unified with the card Temperance, the rune Rad, and the archetypal teacher who possesses an exploratory love for learning, the expansion of ideas, and an insatiable quest to discover new possibilities.

Even though these Jupiterian personalities characteristically have a positive attitude, when troubled, their inner light can dim and create an emotionally distant landscape. Luckily, somewhere in the collective unconscious, they're blessed with a celestial bond to Zeus, the fatherly Roman sky god, who is known to enlighten one's path with transcendental insights, an abundance of good ideas, and tangible expressions of light and love.

Keywords for Sagittarius

The Self
Optimism rules, intelligence, curious minded, professing, philosophical, ambitious, generous, adventurous, a traveler, the explorer

The Shadow
Insensitive, tactless, restless, dogmatic, intolerance, extravagance, can spread one's energy too thin, travel complications

Stirring the Mystic Cauldron

When Divining, These Align with Sagittarius
The card: Temperance
The rune: Rad
The archetype: The teacher

Qualities They Share
Expansion, optimism, philosophy, travel

Capricorn, the Goat

Capricorn, symbolized by a goat with a dolphin tail, is ruled by Saturn, with its celestial connections to ambition, time, karmic lessons, structure, restrictions, responsibilities, duties, obligations, mature perspectives, and old age. Because this sign is the archetypal authoritarian who views virtue as the psyche's guide, people born under its influence have ample opportunity to learn the ethical rules that can help them unravel the knotted cords of their karma and solve deep-seated issues with adversity. Just as mountain goats easily ascend lofty crags, Capricorns are known to skillfully climb cautious steps to higher achievements and soul-liberating vantage points.

Aligned with Chronos, the Greek god of time, who was believed to turn the zodiac wheel of life, Capricorns are naturally inclined to keep a responsible eye on the clock while applying the traits of discipline and concentration to prioritize and realize their goals. Practical, down to earth, and capable, they readily persist and persevere to hone their skills and pursue their earthly desires. Their self-discipline, organizational abilities, and keen understanding of society's rules contribute to their success in becoming authorities in their chosen professions.

The Devil card and the rune Nyd are cosmically connected, so it's understandable that Capricorns can become overly serious about obtaining their goals and toil under high levels of stress. Even though these wise souls are likely to ignore the following advice, it's important to remind them that it's okay to take time to play and sample the pleasures of life.

Keywords for Capricorn

The Self
Goal directed, ambitious, responsible, conscientious, serious, persevering, focused, hard work brings financial opportunity

The Shadow
Overly serious, caution is needed, focus on the wrong instead of the right, needing time off to reset one's intentions

Stirring the Mystic Cauldron

When Divining, These Align with Capricorn
The card: The Devil
The runes: Nyd
The archetype: The authority

Qualities They Share
Focus, finances, responsibility, maturity

Aquarius, the Water Bearer

Aquarius, the sign of the humanitarian, is bonded with the slow-moving, cautious Saturn and the freedom-loving, unpredictable spirit of Uranus. In bygone days, Saturn, associated with karmic lessons, time, self-discipline, concentration, seriousness, and hard work, was considered the sole ruler of Aquarius. But the airy personalities born under this sign have proven themselves to be anything but tied to Saturn's attributes of sticking with tradition, maintaining codes of conduct, and abiding to established rules. With the discovery of Uranus, customary views of the solar system were questioned, and new understanding disrupted the habitual way of looking upward. Over time, it became associated with the expansion of human potential and new ideas on the fringe of normality. Aquarius, aligned with rebelliousness and progressive, visionary thinking, seemed unfit to be tethered in Saturn's structured dominion. After many decades of debate, Uranus became assigned as the perfect copartner for Aquarius.

Linked with the Star card and the rune Mann through their mutual archetype the reformer, the Aquarian New Age thinker is known to work toward improving the wrongs of society. Community minded, they typically strive for universal enrichment through progressive reforms and positive ideals. Curious and friendly, their charisma allows them to readily connect with others, even though some consider this archetype to be a bit threatening because of its "Look me straight in the eye" rebellious nature.

Yet, even if their ideas sometimes question the status quo, they are known to be adept at encouraging others to lend their hands to work for a worthy cause. Sometimes, their nontraditional approach to combating social woes can arouse the more conservative to view them as eccentric. Often while vocalizing positive expectations, they can become overly dogmatic, but who can blame them for searching for sure possibilities for creating utopia on earth.

Keywords for Aquarius

The Self

Community spirited, revolutionary, strives for improvement, deliberate, helpful, open-minded, innovative, independent

The Shadow

Controlling, rebellious, nonconforming, detached, scattered by focusing on too many possibilities

Stirring the Mystic Cauldron

When Divining, These Align with Aquarius

The card: The Star
The rune: Mann
The archetype: The reformer

Qualities They Share

Upbeat, humanitarian, empathy, freedom

Pisces, the Fish

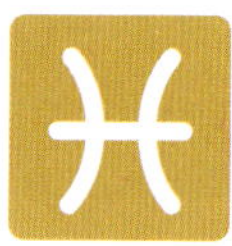

Pisces, the watery sign of two fish swimming in opposite directions, are known to be sensitive to tides of emotional currents swirling in their loving hearts. Even if they sometimes have difficulty making decisions about what direction to go, with their zodiac home being the last, twelfth house on the zodiac wheel, they are usually committed to getting to the finish line and completing what they have begun. Coruled by Jupiter—the planet of wisdom, philosophy, and expansiveness, and Neptune—the hallmark of mysticism, visions, fantasies, and illusion, the Piscean spirit is bound to the creative and intuitive archetype and can be counted on to rise above the ordinary and plunge into the depths of the worlds of dreams and the imagination.

Inspirational when sharing kind words that come naturally, Pisceans seem to float effortlessly in their ocean of emotions without a care in the world. But sometimes, their spirited nature is a disguise to mask their inner complexity. Cosmically tied with the major card The Moon and the rune Hoegl, they share an innate understanding of silent communications and an irresistible attraction to realms beyond the confines of the logical mind.

Empathic and thoughtful, they have an open, friendly nature but can be vulnerable to being called upon to take care of other people's problems. This makes it essential for Pisceans to develop their ability to say "no" so that others don't take advantage of their impressionable nature, even if they may be inspired to alleviate suffering. When their energy is constructively channeled, they are known to write poetry and music and dance with ecstatic abandon. As the zodiac caretaker of lost souls, they mostly have a can-do attitude that enables them to achieve visible results for their actions and deftly sight dolphins and whales jumping on the ocean's waves.

Keywords for Pisces

The Self
Changeable, intuitive, receptive, sensitive, emotional, generous, dependable, buoyant, imaginative, dreamy

The Shadow
Overly emotional, indecisive, moody, insecure, gullible, tearfully sensitive, anger prompts tears

When Divining, These Align with Pisces
The card: The Moon
The rune: Hoegl
The archetype: The intuitive

Qualities They Share
Imagination, instinct, understanding, caring

EXPLORING THE PLANETS

 The Sun

The sun, planet Earth's closest star, inspires the radiant power of light, growth, regeneration, and healing. A shining representative for the male principle, it is equaled with yang energy, the father, masculine energy, heroes, individuality, authority, and confidence. In ancient times its life-giving force was worshiped as Apollo, a Greek and Roman sun deity with prophetic and healing attributes, who was considered the source of creation and the dazzling escort to spring.

Vitality and passion complement the personal experiences that are intensified by the sun's glowing warmth. With attributes comparable to qualities inherently found in the Sun card and the rune Sigel, it's associated with the archetype of the self, conscious awareness, healing inspirations, and the power of positive thinking.

Wherever the sun sits on your chart reveals the area where your natural resources can be mined for health, success, and individualism. For example, if your natal chart sun sits in the second house, associated with the earthiness of Taurus, personal ambition, and financial desire, your energy to reach your financial goals will glow and grow in its light. The brilliance transmitted from this orb can even filter through dark clouds to enlighten and clarify a path that takes one from shadows to status.

Keywords for the Sun

The Self
Solar-creative energy, positive forces of light, children, growth, happiness, love, vitality, authority, prosperity of spirit

The Shadow
Diminished light or authority, emerging shadows or dark energy, arrogance, blocks in love, selfishness, self-indulgence

When Divining, These Align with the Sun
The card: The Sun
The rune: Sigel
The archetype: The self

Qualities They Share
Vitality, creativity, children, happiness

 Moon

Lunar reflections of solar light illuminate the nocturnal depth of the psyche, where memories, dreams, imagination, and intuition make their home. Mythologically equated with the archetype of the divine maiden, the moon shines on the beauty in the Wiccan trinity: the maiden, the mother, and the crone. Each face in this ethereal trio represents a different goddess, a distinct phase of the moon, and an evolutionary stage of womanhood.

This maiden dances in the growing energy of the waxing moon. She is equaled with the naive Greek goddess Persephone, who was kidnapped by the horned god Hades and taken to his underground kingdom. Her mother, the goddess Demeter, second goddess in the mystic trio, went into the underworld desperately heartbroken to plea for her daughter's release. Because the adorable maiden had been seduced to taste the sweetness of six pomegranate seeds offered by Hades, she was bound to his decree. After much debate between Hades and Demeter, he let his abducted lover go back to Earth as long as she promised to return to his home to be his queen for six months of the year, one month for each seed that she had tasted.

Hecate, also associated with Artemis, goddess of the witches, is the third goddess in the trine. A crone and wise woman, she works magic beyond the logical mind and trains students in the psychic arts. Her heart is a temple for the High Priestess card and transformational matters related to the rune Is. To honor and navigate the up-and-down currents of life, the moon unfreezes the sway of tides in subconscious realms and releases chilled emotions to spill beyond their boundaries. In current times, you can often spot adventurous moon maidens on the beach, wearing bikinis with their surfboards in tow.

Keywords for the Moon

The Self
The feminine, the subconscious, intuition, dreams, imagination, raw emotions, moodiness, esoterica, travel, waves of change

The Shadow
Mommy issues, mean-spirited emotions, mood swings, manipulation, domestic concerns, gullibility

Stirring the Mystic Cauldron

When Divining, These Align with the Moon
The card: The High Priestess
The rune: Is
The archetype: The maiden

Qualities They Share
The feminine, esoterica, nurturing, dreams

PHASES OF THE MOON

The Waxing Moon

New moon: This is a perfect time to learn to develop your intuitive skills. Waves of emotions grow stronger, and you may feel inspired to create a vision board for affirming your dreams for future accomplishments. If you plant seeds in your mind with affirmations or prayers, or by vocalizing intentions, and put forth needed effort, it can accelerate the sprouting of desired, new beginnings. What has been out of sight may come into view with an increase of lunar light.

First-quarter moon: With an increase in light and energy, the energy being directed after planting ideas during the new moon becomes stronger. Vitality mixes with hope for success to bring a flow of enthusiasm to the surface, and the heart may beat with a more optimistic rhythm.

Full moon: This time of maximum lunar light heightens reflective awareness. If you want to dive deeply into the why and why not of any situation, you'll be able to find bright illuminations as you submerge into the depth of your being. Because emotions surge with higher waves than at other times, be prepared. Not a time for superficial speculation, since even lighthearted matters can trigger unexpected emotional insights within.

Keywords for the Waxing Moon

The Self
Psychic strength, positive changes, increase in clarity, planting seeds of the power to succeed, the home gets attention

The Shadow
Ignoring your instincts, connecting with your vulnerable emotions, the heart speaks openly, questioning choices

Stirring the Mystic Cauldron

When Divining, These Align with the Waxing Moon
The card: The High Priestess
The rune: Ethel
The archetype: The active maiden

Qualities They Share
Property, depth, memories, clairvoyance

The Waning Moon

Third lunar phase: It's a good time to assess plans and work with the energies initiated during waxing lunar cycles, but the moon's light is decreasing and its ebbing tides lessen spirited reflections. Invoke your psychic focus to be steady on your divinatory path and enlist your intuitive awareness. Even rational energy may need to be disciplined so you stay on track and don't get distracted from your priorities.

Last-quarter moon: It's the perfect time for planting nightshades in the garden of your life and weeding out pessimism from your dreams. Logic speaks louder than intuition. Emotions may heighten moods, making the likes of a ride on Cinderella's pumpkin coach at midnight look like a smooth spin.

Dark of the moon: With the absence of lunar light comes the time for meditation, repose, and conserving emotional energy. Low tides of worldly energy may have an impact on instinctive common sense. It's not a safe time to gamble with passionate ideas and the good fortune that you may have gained during the waxing moon.

Keywords for the Waning Moon

The Self
Critical-mindedness, lower-than-normal vitality, changing your mind, feminine issues may surface

The Shadow
Moody, self-esteem needs a boost, feelings may be emotionally or intuitively off-center, needing to deal with domestic issues

When Divining, These Align with the Waning Moon
The card: The High Priestess
The rune: Thorn
The archetype: The passive maiden

Qualities They Share
Challenge, oppression, taboo, travel

Mercury

Even though small in physical size, this sphere plays a giant role as the symbolic avatar over conscious thought, the power of ideas, the expression of words, and the vitality of the nervous system. Associated with linear logic, Mercury embraces intelligence, communication, speaking, writing, magic, science, technology, networking, and healing. Sharing its name with the Roman god who had wings on his feet, it was known as Hermes to the ancient Greeks, the messenger for the gods. He is often portrayed carrying the caduceus, the long-established medical symbol for healers. You may see this winged staff entwined with two snakes on windows or doors of doctors, therapists, midwives, and those who offer healing care.

In his archetypal role as healer, Mercury is honored for the uncanny ability to perceive divine insights and channel healing to humanity. Associated with the Magician card and the rune Os, the insights that it brings can be subtle or intense, overt or covert, and normally loaded with useful insights for well-being and personal empowerment. Being perceptive to the ideas of others and having a quickness of thought often gives those who possess Mercurial energy a leading edge in their professional field and the know-how to communicate in a timely fashion.

Connected with the youthful spirit that never grows old, their mindset includes a restlessness that stirs interest for travel, the invention of new things, and the desire to create futuristic projects. Ultimately, its Mercurial insights clarify ideas and harvest common sense for looking rationally into the meanings of the stars, cards, and stones.

Keywords for Mercury

The Self
Ideas, keen perceptions, discrimination, critical-mindedness, versatility, powerful communication, writing, networking, travel

The Shadow
Blocked communication, cynicism, intolerance, scattered or wasted mental energy, nervousness, impatience

Stirring the Mystic Cauldron

When Divining, These Align with Mercury
The card: The Magician
The rune: Os
The archetype: The healer

Qualities They Share
Communication, travel, youthfulness, magic

Venus

A benefic planet, Venus is identified with artistic inspiration that fills one's heart with pleasurable pursuits, such as romance, music, drama, and dance. Marriage, loving commitments, magnetic relations, seduction, and physical lust are also Venusian affairs. It is associated with Aphrodite, the Greek goddess of love, who is reputed to bestow earthly opportunities for passion, flirting, fertility, peace, and finding beauty. Her son Eros, gorgeous and loving like his mother, is known to be bighearted and loyal. By overcoming challenges in forbidden love, he became the mythic hero who proved to the collective that it's possible to prevail over obstacles on the path of true love.

As love's archetype, the ancient Greek god Eros is the manifestation of the willful passion to engage in physical intimacy and touch the heat of one's emotions. Another face of love's seduction, celebrated for his powers to incite lustful desire, is Cupid, the Romans' god of love, notorious for shooting arrows into unsuspecting hearts to get their passion flowing. Attributes identified with these gods, such as the enjoyment of pleasure and romance, are central in the interpretations given to the Empress card and the runestone Beorc. You can look at the placement of Venus in someone's natal chart to see where his arrows hit the mark of romantic possibilities.

Positive characteristics ascribed to Venus are harmony and the heightening of emotional sensitivity, sensuality, and compatible sociability. Its negative attributes are vanity, selfish love, and the gluttony of a pleasure-seeking, hedonistic lifestyle. But even if people blame the charms of Venus on their addiction to love, it is known mostly for encouraging happy relations, playful pleasures, and enjoyment of the humanities.

Keywords for Venus

The Self
Fulfillment, beauty, harmony, love, desire, sensuality, passion, pleasures, passionate pursuits, music, and other arts

The Shadow
Vanity, emotional immaturity, discordant emotions, overthinking emotions, artistic issues, eroticism

Stirring the Mystic Cauldron

When Divining, These Align with Venus
The card: The Empress
The rune: Beorc
The archetype: Eros

Qualities They Share
Love, beauty, pleasure, happiness

Mars

Mars, the red planet, is analogous with physical vitality, stamina, virility, athletics, action, confidence, and sexual energy. Adventurous, assertive, and often authoritative, its fierce warrior archetype is birthed from strong will, passion, and a deep-rooted sense of righting societies' wrongs. Regardless of possessing the heroic courage to face the enemy, Mars's robust nature can turn angry and antagonistic when adrenaline is surging.

Mythic stories calling out the aggressive nature of the Roman god of war, Mars, who shares this planet's name, give clues to the qualities that have given life to its malefic reputation. Ignoring the demands of its fiery energy can take one on a time-wasting detour, because turning away from its heat can make it burn hotter and rage out of control. Its untamed power is also visible in its corresponding card The Tower and the rune Feoh. Learning to cool the battle cries of its sometimes overheated energy is one of the lessons that can be necessary for those who have Mars dominant in their birth chart. Yet, it is this same level of intensity that can ignite one's willingness to jump into a burning building to save someone's life.

Fortunately, when the positive energy of Mars is harnessed, progress to any desired goal can quickly accelerate. This enduring energy is active, passionate, and willing to fight offensively or defensively to achieve success. When uplifting qualities are combined with the high drive, motivation, and the resourceful spirit related to Mars, life's challenges can be easily faced, and debates won with a smile.

Keywords for Mars

The Self
Assertiveness, fiery action, physical drive, stamina, strength, sexual energy, willpower, competition, forceful persuasion, courage

The Shadow
Power struggles, stubbornness, anger, detachment, war, weakened physical drive or stamina

Stirring the Mystic Cauldron

When Divining, These Align with Mars
The card: The Tower
The rune: Feoh
The archetype: The initiator

Qualities They Share
Action, confrontation, competition, autonomy

♃ Jupiter

In Greek and Roman mythologies, Jupiter was the supreme god and father of the sky, who upheld cosmic order and oversaw all aspects of life. Because of his ubiquitous popularity, he was compared to the largest visible planet in the heavens. Able to explore the depths of sea and psyche, he had an instinct to know truth from lies, attain lofty ideals, and uphold just laws over lawlessness.

Equal with its majestic mythic roots, this planet is mortally tied to wisdom, philosophy, religion, spiritual aspirations, the guru, optimism, wealth, and ambition. It aligns with the archetypal force of the explorer who is willing to wander to every corner of the world, from the highest mountain to the bottom of the sea, in search of opportunities to expand awareness, wealth, and good fortune. As virtuous and generous as this warmhearted personality can be, unless prudent such a person can still fall prey to being overly optimistic, overly indulgent, self-absorbed, egocentric, and extravagant.

Because Jupiter rules over working in governments, politics, lecturing, higher education, and advertising, it has a strong influence over society and its norms. Fortunately, its reputed curious, positive nature is known to facilitate growth, progress, and personal enrichment. It shares its auspicious attributes with the Wheel of Fortune card and the auspicious rune Wynn. Wherever it appears on one's chart, it brings an uplifting quality to one's personal evolution and a green light to move toward finding fulfillment.

Keywords for Jupiter

The Self
Philosophy, justice, wisdom, education, expansion, progress, ambition, success in business, good fortune, generosity, travel

The Shadow
Extravagance, self-interest, unwise spending or investing, insensitivity, reliance on chance instead of good sense

Stirring the Mystic Cauldron

When Divining, These Align with Jupiter
The card: The Wheel of Fortune
The rune: Wynn
The archetype: The explorer

Qualities They Share
Expansion, foresight, positivity, winning

Saturn

Saturn is linked with economy, boundaries, restriction, conservatism, and wisdom learned through experience. It is bonded with the ancient Greek god Cronus, or Old Father Time, with his grating scythe, who brought the passing of time, maturity, old age, and important lessons to help people learn right from wrong. Without fail and having all the time in creation, he had one eye on the clock and moved through the world to help humanity overcome their ignorance and learn respect for the rules of right living.

Saturn embodies the timekeeper and archetypal wise elder who teaches the discerning knowledge inspirited in the last major card, The World, and the rune Peordh. Personified as the ultimate authority, Saturn aligns with the philosophy of karma, the not-for-the-fainthearted universal law that each person reaps what he or she sows. Biblically confirmed by Luke the Evangelist, who considered actions to create reactions, it implies that whatever you give determines what you receive. Either positive or negative, the energy that people send into creation, like a boomerang, comes back in some equivalent form.

Saturn represents the stern teacher who points to the lessons each one of us is destined to experience. Through his hand of discipline, we are encouraged to open our eyes to view the skeletal foundation of our strengths and weaknesses, even if we try to flee from our moral responsibility to learn right from wrong and correct mistakes.

Opposite Jupiter's expansive energy, Saturn inspires constrictive, orderly, methodical, and conservative efforts. Associated with limitations, confinement, lawsuits, melancholy, discipline, and mature thinking, it's not always a welcomed guest at fun-loving parties. Even so, most of us can become uplifted with its positive qualities of forgiveness, sincerity, concentration, and longevity, which offer an unequaled opportunity to grow wiser and improve our worldly and spiritual conditions.

Keywords for Saturn

The Self
Karma, law of cause and effect, lessons, overcoming constraints or restrictions, taking responsibility, hard work, concentration

The Shadow
Need for discipline, fear of aging, wrongful confinement, setbacks, going against the rules, detours from harmony

Stirring the Mystic Cauldron

When Divining, These Align with Saturn
The card: The World
The Rune: Peordh
The archetype: The wise elder

Qualities They Share
Karma, values, responsibility, limits

Uranus

Uranus—abnormal, erratic, and obscure—is a planet with qualities that include extremism, nonconformity, altruism, freedom of thought, thinking outside the box, originality, individuality, and inventiveness. It inspires the eccentric, the libertarian, and the revolutionary, all of whom live beyond the common boundaries imposed by society.

Comparable with the archetypal child—and teenager, and the Fool card and the rune Daeg, Uranus is associated with breaking the tethers of conditioning and pursuing spontaneity of mind, body, spirit. With this popular universal archetype, the phrase "Expect the unexpected" rises to a state of its ultimate actuality. Like a flower blooming on the battlefield of transmutation, Uranus is a soothing balm to the necessary growing pains that bring about positive change with a few small but, most often, profound adjustments.

In some circumstances, its energy can be compared with the heart of struggles during times when a child is told "No" by the parent, and the child's mood swiftly changes from love to anger or from pleasure to pain in one high-speed pendulum swing. To stir the thoughts of responsibility, Uranus, the advocating voice for swift improvement and the orator for unexpected reality checks, brings stuck feelings from the invisible depths of the psyche to the surface. With a little push toward evolving awareness, the silent power of the mind can transform the Uranus shake-up into an inspiring state of liberation that nudges one to awaken to a dawning light on reformed beginnings, meaningful ventures, intuition, and positive growth.

Keywords for Uranus

The Self
The unexpected, extremes, advocate for positive change, sudden alterations in mood, nonconformity, startling insights, reform tactics

The Shadow
Eccentricity, alchemy, detachment from the norm, radical activities, rioting, rebellion, lack of agreements

Stirring the Mystic Cauldron

When Divining, These Align with Uranus
The card: The Fool
The rune: Daeg
The archetype: The child

Qualities They Share
The unexpected, freedom, innovation, unrest

Neptune

Astrologically speaking, Neptune is equal to illusion, dreams, visions, intuition, and the playful spirit of the imagination. Psilocybin, marijuana, hallucinogens, and other drugs are under its rulership, as are the euphoria, addiction, and paraphernalia that can accompany them. Radio, TV, movies, and other things that create a virtual playground for the imagination and alter perceptions of reality, such as video productions and camera art, are also connected to its influence.

Looking at this planet in connection with Roman mythology, its wisdom can be compared with the temperamental god Neptune, the god of the sea, who carried a trident. In ancient Greece he was popularly known as Poseidon. Depending on his mood, he could create calm or storm within his domain and affect the up-and-down sways in the sea of earthly matters involving boating, ships, and sailors. Metaphorically, he is comparable to the misty fog that floats effortlessly from the sea, distorting visual acuity and passively altering perceptions of reality.

If you are a psychic, create poetry, or write musical lyrics, some might say that you have an intimate connection with Neptunian energy. Vision quests, spiritual pilgrimages, and martyrdom linked with the Hanged Man card and the rune Lagu also exist under the open umbrella of its allure. Its nonlinear, instinctive qualities are why Neptune's archetype is comparable to the mystic, who is known to be sensitive, impressionistic, and awake in the world of dreams. If talking with God is an illusion, this archetype, who is sublimely tied to the compassionate, spiritual soul, can help turn such a conversation into a discernible truth.

When not protecting their open-to-life nature, Neptune personalities can be lured by charlatans and fall prey to deceitful lies or fantasies without realizing that they are becoming prey to fraudulent rewards. Even so, Neptune has a celestially aligned reputation for influencing inspirational energy and stellar creative, visionary, and psychic endeavors.

Keywords for Neptune

The Self
Dreams, visions, watery, subtle forces, seeing intuitively, the synchronicity, mystical or spiritual pursuits, virtual reality, video games

The Shadow
Unrealistic dreams, exaggeration, scheming, delusion, insecurities, avoidance, drugs, addiction to love

Stirring the Mystic Cauldron

When Divining, These Align with Neptune	Qualities They Share
The card: The Hanged Man The rune: Lagu The archetype: The mystic	Dreams, illusion, intuition, nonconformity

Pluto

Pluto, the planet farthest from our sun, is named after the Greek god of the underworld, Hades, who boldly kidnapped the young maiden Persephone to make her queen of his underworld. Reputed to be malefic yet sublime, this orb often leaves a wake of confusion because it's a sign both of death and birth, decay and regeneration. The soul-stirring rebirth associated with the Judgement card and the rune Ing forces us to wake up to the importance of letting go of the old, worn, and useless—even if we don't want to detach from their comforts. With a little luck from auspicious fate, the destruction of the familiar can accelerate a renaissance in awareness that brings opportunities for improvement and advancement. We can either accept and surrender to its influences and move forward with an open mind or fight the inevitable.

Often talked about with reference to the dark night of the soul, or visions from the past that suddenly surface from the subconscious with a jolt, it can initiate a mental tumble and fall. Those things that lie forgotten in a forbidding maze of memories may unexpectedly demand your renewed attention and deep reflection.

The harbinger of guilt and shame and things that are hidden from view, such as kidnapping, murder, sexual misconduct, and unsolvable crimes, Pluto's presence can feel a bit threatening to one's inner peace. On a brighter note, it is also reputed to illuminate subtle connections and secret pathways to unrealized potentials. Tied to the invisible but powerful undercurrent of group genius and unconscious activities that may effect change in the collective, it nonchalantly mingles or messes with social perceptions. Offering a hand to tickle the underbelly of the world, it shifts the evolutionary gears of generational karma. Simply stated, an encounter with Pluto is not to be taken lightly.

Keywords for Pluto

The Self
Transformation, metamorphosis, unexpected outbursts, renewal after conflict, power to influence, karma, breaking commitments

The Shadow
Depression, obsessions, tears, exploring unfamiliar depths, manipulation, feeling out of tune, pressure to change, temptation

Stirring the Mystic Cauldron

When Divining, These Align with Pluto
The card: Judgement
The rune: Ing
The archetype: Rebirth

Qualities They Share
Transformation, disruption, the subconscious, mystery

CHAPTER 7

MEETING THE TWENTY-TWO MAJOR ARCANA

Newsworthy Notes

The Tarot's pathway is an exploration of consciousness, with a close-up view of the world of spirit and the material realms of finances, love, power, enterprise, and passion. Whatever deck you are using, as long as you like it, is perfect for this study. The major card illustrations and accompanying discussions can benefit your Tarot journey no matter what deck you are using.

Aligning Tarot with Astrology

The correspondences between the Tarot and the zodiac that are used here are adopted from a divinatory system developed by the secret society known as the Hermetic Order of the Golden Dawn. This influential magical order existed in the late 1800s and early 1900s. Their popular Tarot-astrological correlations can be found in many contemporaneous books and have influenced many readers learning astrology and its connections with the Tarot.

Keyword Headings

Upright card meanings are listed under the heading titled "The Self."

Reversed cards are listed under the heading "The Shadow."

These lists are to help you build your foundation of interpretative meanings and to encourage your efforts to give Tarot readings. The meanings for the cards are as numerous as there are people reading them. As you progress with your Tarot studies, your interpretations will become more personal and most likely will expand with your understanding of what, why, and how their meanings relate to your personal understanding of symbols.

Justice and Strength

If you're wondering why your deck has the Justice card numbered 8 instead of 11, it's easy to explain. Before Arthur Waite cocreated his Rider-Waite deck in 1910, Justice held the eighth position and Strength was numbered 11 in the Major Arcana's sequence. Your personal deck's placement of these cards is accurate in accord with the belief of your deck's creator(s). Both numeric systems are in current use today. As you play with your cards, you're likely to become sensitive to subliminal clues and veiled messages within your deck that will act as arrows pointing to the best system for you to use.

Gender

In current times, with a focus on gender equality, you can find Tarot decks with images that reverse the accustomed male and female roles and commentaries. Currently, my deck collection has several decks that have 100 percent feminine forms, and some decks have only masculine figures (yes, The Magician can be female and The High Priestess can be masculine, for example). If you are using a gender-specific deck, when feasible please substitute its gender framework within my discussions.

DISCOVERING THE MAGIC IN THE MAJOR ARCANA

1. The Magician
Also called the Juggler, the Alchemist, and the Magus

The Magician, the first Major Arcana card, is linked with taking the first steps on the journey toward developing higher consciousness. Associated with the archetypal healer called Hermes in ancient Greece and the god Mercury in Rome, he embodies the one-pointedness of mind needed to awaken from the slumber in which you have forgotten your personal magic and how to use it. As you remember and begin to develop it, he stands before you as a role model to guide you to ignite self-mastery, learn to heal yourself and others, and experience greater knowing of your earthly mission.

The young man dressed in flowing robes of white—the color of pure intention, innocence, and perfection—reflects an otherworldly confidence and determination. Standing in front of his ceremonial altar, he shows by his stance the determination to transcend the limits of the finite world. True to magical practices, his one arm points toward the heavens and the other toward the earth, bodily illustrating the Hermetic maxim "As above, so below." His power to apply this knowledge will be tested when he uses his alchemical skills to channel the wisdom of the macrocosm to the Grail-thirsty souls on Earth.

The golden light shining through his third eye, doorway to spiritual communion, shows that he is aligned with the eternal flame of soul illumination. As he uses his fiery wand to balance the forces of duality, the light and the dark, the masculine and the feminine, the sweet and the sour, part of his task is to access the ways he can convince you to follow the "Fool's Journey" that lies before those who are bold enough to believe in the power of Tarot's magic.

Keywords for The Magician

The Self
Magic, swift thinking, originality, charisma, focus, communication, persuasiveness, writing, psychic channeling, travel

The Shadow
Not owning the power of your ideas, the need to take responsibility for your decisions, blocked communication, procrastination

Stirring the Mystic Cauldron

When Divining, These Align with The Magician
The planet: Mercury
The rune: Os
The archetype: The healer

Qualities They Share
Communication, travel, youthful, magic

2. The High Priestess
Also called the Female Pope and Isis Veiled

The High Priestess wears a crescent moon over the middle of her forehead, gateway to communication with the divine and home of the all-seeing third eye. Her dazzling brilliance casts light on mastery over material conflicts and worries. Centered in her core, she is not agitated by the waxing-waning, positive-negative forces in the world. Balanced between light and darkness, she seems to be dreaming of healing the suffering of humanity while sitting stoically in front of the veil of Maya or illusion. Moods, emotions, and desires pass through her as vibrations, but they fail to impede her peaceful heart because she dwells in the superconscious domain beyond the logic of the five senses.

Journeying through the nighttime sky, this divine maiden hears truth without words being spoken, and feels sympathy for those caught in the complexities of mundane life.

Wearing an invisible protective psychic shield, she guards the locked doorway to eternal mysteries that opens only for initiates who seek the highest arcane degree.

Through the cards and the stones, she shares the magic of her oracular skills with those who seek to learn her ways to help others.

In many decks, this archetypal maiden holds the sacred scrolls of the divine feminine and wisdom of the ancient sages. Thought by some to be the Tora, analogous to the Torah, the ancient Hebrew Pentateuch or Five Books of Moses, its sacred pages reflect both conscious and subconscious energy shifting from the twilight of darkness to the dawning of awakening. Sometimes compared with the goddess of compassion, Kwan Yin, and such lunar deities as Jana, Selene, and Artemis, the High Priestess is celebrated for seeing with an unfaltering owllike vision the instinctual truths that are often overlooked in the light of day.

Keywords for The High Priestess

The Self
The power of the feminine, balancing the ebb and flow of emotions, sensitive issues, reconciling dualities, subconscious insights

The Shadow
Dominant emotional struggles, escaping problems, ambiguous feelings, insecurity, veiled changes of the heart

Stirring the Mystic Cauldron

When Divining, These Align with The High Priestess
The planet: The moon
The rune: Is
The archetype: The maiden

Qualities They Share
The feminine, esoterica, nurturing, dreams

The High Priestess symbolizes both the waxing/active and waning/passive lunar cycles and the moon's widespread connections with magic, mystery, and ritual. For more information, go to the following:

***For the waxing moon, chapter 6, the Moon, and chapter 8, the rune Ethel
***For the waning moon, chapter 6, the Moon, and chapter 8, the rune Thorn

3. The Empress
Also called the Queen, Isis, Isis Unveiled

The Empress dances with the catalysts of positive forces, productivity, creativity, and happiness. Equaled with the planet Venus, she personifies the glow of both inner and outer beauty, the flow of emotions, protection of the heart, and a shield of unfaltering love. Like Venus, the Roman goddess of beauty, she smiles her compassionate grin while being surrounded by a garden of earthly bounty. Her calm poise communicates a message of concern, affection, and kindness for all. Flowers circle the face of The Empress like an aura that manifests the fertile blessings of Mother Earth. Sharing her glory, the archetypal Eros looks out through her eyes, asking you to become the love you seek. Silently smiling, she holds the elemental miracles of God's creations in her hands. From her hand, the icon for the planet Venus glows like a star, rising from the ebbing and flowing sea of emotions from deep within the celestial temple of the female psyche. The booming voice calling from her silent heart declares her authority in the realm of sensual matters.

The mature aspect of fertility, she symbolizes the evolutionary wisdom of the feminine, who dances with the mysteries of life-birthing forces and the nativity of creation. Her penetrating gaze personifies the glory of the love songs of nature and the willingness to open the heart. She is comparable to Demeter, Gaia, Freyja, and other goddesses, and her dialogue combines the awakening of spring, the sprouting of life-giving seeds, and the fruitfulness of the harvest. When you feel her gifts of grace, compassion, and mercy, she's sure to help you find your path to happiness.

Keywords for The Empress

The Self

Abundance, joy, fertility, love, marriage, pregnancy, friendships, uplifting the mind and emotions, tolerance, healing of the earth

The Shadow

A troubled friendship, emotional coldness, confusion or stress, insecurities, being unproductive, stifled creativity

Stirring the Mystic Cauldron

When Divining, These Align with The Empress

The planet: Venus
The rune: Beorc
The archetype: Eros

Qualities They Share

Love, beauty, pleasure, happiness

4. The Emperor
Also called the Sultan and the Governor

A noble ruler with a dark beard sits on a stone throne, holding his hand in the shape of a scepter of worldly awareness. He looks out over the land, confident in his mastery of earthly matters. He typifies universal wisdom, fatherly authority, logic, and financial know-how.

The historical role of an emperor is as the sovereign head of an empire. The card that bears this title likewise indicates a man with dominion, leadership, and power. Possessing fiery qualities linked with supreme power, his image is comparable to the archetypal god of war, Ares, who typifies power, physical stamina, and the willingness to initiate action and face confrontation when necessary. As an advocate for those he rules, when worst comes to worst, he uses his sword and social stance to ensure people's safety and survival.

When near his partner, The Empress (Major Arcana 3), he can soften his tough exterior to typify the passionate lover who usually keeps his emotions in check—although he can sometimes become enraged. Even when enjoying his privileges as the monarch, he may still remain a dutiful husband with strong paternal instincts.

A symbol of the masculine principle, he represents positive, yang power that completes and complements yin, feminine energy. With the force of a ram, he energizes the unbridled powers of the intellect, reason, and the virtue of volition.

Keywords for The Emperor

The Self

Wisdom, power, assertiveness, fiery energy, prestige, dominance, a rebirth of opportunity, executing a plan for greater prosperity

The Shadow

A power struggle or manipulative situation, faulty leadership, being overly demanding, having too many goals, financial worries

Stirring the Mystic Cauldron

When Divining, These Align with The Emperor

The sun sign: Aries
The rune: Tyr
The archetype: The leader

Qualities They Share

Strong will, ambition, courage, independence

5. The High Priest
Also called The Hierophant

Sitting between two mountains, the high priest, crowned with a five-pointed star of spiritual initiation, appears to be in a trance in a remote space where the earth meets the heavens. Wearing the enchanting robes of the shaman, an icon for Taurus, the bull sits on his right, denoting his connection with ancient myths and the higher laws of arcane knowledge. A bear sits on his left, symbolizing the determination needed to transcend the tethers of mortal challenges and fated whirlpools of destiny. With the steadfast gaze of a bull ready to charge, he has invoked the spellbinding pentagram to appear beneath his feet and point the way to supernatural consciousness.

During the times of the Eleusinian mysteries, the high priest presided over sacred rites and temples where locked doors kept the esoteric mysteries safe from prying, unqualified eyes. In modern times, his archetypal role is equated with the shamanic quest to find the center of the labyrinth, where the mundane becomes sacred. Grounded by his link with the earth element, most often his worldly purpose is to shine a light on yet-to-be-discovered truths that can remove the heaviness of perplexing difficulties.

His connection with Venus, the ruler of Taurus, reminds his viewers to remember to focus on love and light while developing their divinatory abilities. Similar to this hierophant, we too can knock on the doorway to infinite possibilities and apply our efforts to becoming masters of mind over matter. Sensitive to vibrational energy, he shines light on using your intuition, meditative communication with the higher self, and tapping into the healing-heart energy of compassion. His teachings remind us to keep an open-minded awareness of our sixth sense in order to delve into nonlinear insights and trust our nonverbal conversations with the oracles.

Keywords for The High Priest

The Self
Truth, spiritual or intuitive awareness, a meeting with a spiritual master or master craftsperson, understanding one's purpose, pursuit of happiness

The Shadow
Broken commitments, dogmatism, corrupt leadership, confusion, conflict of values, distraction from priorities

Stirring the Mystic Cauldron

When Divining, These Align with The High Priest
The sun sign: Taurus
The rune: Ur
The archetype: The shaman

Qualities They Share
Determination, fertility, stability, affection

6. The Lovers
Also called Choice and the Two Paths

A ray of light extending from the heavens illuminates a man and woman locked in a euphoric embrace. When viewing these Lovers, we hear the poetry of the heart being silently sung. The kiss and the rapture of the moment bring to mind the light of twin flames merging into one. The sharing of their passion is visually bold, like the innate power of the heart to communicate its message laden with emotions without saying even one word.

The couple, who can be viewed as male-logical and female-intuitive archetypal messengers of the birth of humanity, knowingly or unknowingly stand next to the Tree of Knowledge of Good and Evil. Its vibrant green foliage brings to mind the Garden of Eden and the biblical creation myth of Adam and Eve, who lived in a paradise before the serpent of temptation caused their banishment. As the religiously celebrated first man and woman, father and mother, husband and wife, they are the positive-solar-masculine and negative-lunar-feminine representatives of complementary opposites.

In a wordless manner, the wisdom being communicated through this card suggests that we pay attention to the song of love playing a vibrational melody in our hearts. What romantic dreams should we strive to fulfill? Do we accept others as they are or try to remake them as we'd prefer that they be? How can we best find our bliss and be happy in our complex lives? Like twins juggling choices of either being independent or standing together as one, or to toss the runes or shuffle the cards, it's our decision whether to keep our hearts and psyches open or to shelter them protectively.

Keywords for Thc Lovers

The Self
Inspiration, intimate communication, union of opposites, self-love vs. partnership, collaboration, emotional insights, appropriate choices

The Shadow
Blocked communications, not honoring another's needs, feelings of separateness, difficult choices, temptation

Stirring the Mystic Cauldron

When Divining, These Align with The Lovers
The sun sign: Gemini
The rune: Eh
The archetype: The messenger

Qualities They Share
Unity, messages, choices, duality

7. Chariot
Also called Victory and the Conqueror

The charioteer, aligned with the protector, drives his celestial coach by means of two winged horses, one black and one white. These reflect the polarity of yoni (female, negative) and lingam (male, positive) energy. Each pegasi mythically gallops between birth and death, tugging in opposite directions while pulling their coach toward an overdue meeting with higher intelligence. Without reins, but with the intuition and sensitivities characteristic of the watery Cancerians, the charioteer steers safely across the River of Life, reducing the fear of life's uncertain currents and moving toward a winning destiny.

Wearing a garment decorated with magical and astrological signs, the driver shows alignment with Artemis, the Greek lunar goddess of the hunt and favored keeper of esoteric disciplines. The eight-pointed star crowning the driver's third eye indicates that he has worked hard to become a guide for those seeking to merge with the eternal flame of the cosmic matrix. The victory garland is a sign of honoring one's wisdom to stand strong against disturbing forces of duality, doubt, or intimidation.

Vehicle of the ancient gods, this supernatural chariot covered with a canopy of twinkling stars is being driven in a realm beyond logical understanding. Its wheels spiral forward over the bumps on the roads of circumstance, seeking the way to the heart's home. Aligned with the archetypal nurturer, this charioteer advocates being in service to others and developing self-control over vacillating waves of emotional ups and downs. If you are in a situation where you feel strongly pulled in two different directions, listening to your truth's wisdom can help you navigate the unknown and know the right way to go.

Keywords for The Chariot

The Self
Intuitive awareness, persistence, peak performance, being nurtured, making the right choice, opportunities to advance, protection

The Shadow
Ambivalence stirs uncertainty, feeling vulnerable, avoiding emotional issues, work is needed, slow-moving wheels of progress

Stirring the Mystic Cauldron

When Divining, These Align with The Chariot
The sun sign: Cancer
The rune: Eolh
The archetype: The nurturer

Qualities They Share
Receptivity, protection, change, clairvoyance

8. Strength
Also called Fortitude and Fire

This sorceress, who wears long, flowing robes, has completed her initiation of sacred rites at the Eye of Horus Mystery School. She understands the sacred art of ritual and knows how to use her physical energy to activate spiritual and mental powers. Assuming the role of enchantress, this magical mistress has taken a giant leap on her path to mastering her ability to channel the Light.

Holding two lotus flowers demonstrates her innocence, her self-control, and a keen sensitivity to nature. The trident in her lap, representing will, knowledge, and action, makes it apparent that her journey includes meandering through the dimly lit corridors of the superconscious mind to raise the Kundalini or Shakti energy coiled at the base of her spine.

Comparable to the Egyptian goddess Isis and the Hindu goddess Durga, this solar sorceress possesses the wisdom, desire, and capability to control the untamed forces that could devour her. Without showing fear, this archetypal enchantress sits next to the exotic beast, which normally exhibits a wild nature with unbridled fierceness.

With the same courage she demonstrates by befriending the tiger, she stands and beckons you to harness your fiery will to channel the alluring forces of your courage, talents, and creativity. Empowered with magnetic charisma and tenderheartedness, her awakened wisdom calls upon you to connect with your inner light and join her in giving the best of what you can offer to the world.

Keywords for Strength

The Self

Owning your power, fiery strength, courage, strong instincts, happiness, creative or productive efforts, developing your talents

The Shadow

Confidence needs rebuilding, darkness overshadows positive thinking, the need to own your power

Stirring the Mystic Cauldron

When Divining, These Align with Strength

The sun sign: Leo
The rune: Cen
The archetype: The enchanter

Qualities They Share

Vitality, boldness, heroism, happiness

9. The Hermit
Also called Wisdom of Earth and the Prophet

Wearing a hooded cloak, a solitary person stands in the mist on a lofty mountain. He's portrayed as the archetypal sage who holds the staff of knowledge, guidance, and healing associated with the Roman god Mercury, known as Hermes in Greek myths. Since this hermit's staff is held in his right hand, it is physically directed by the left hemisphere of the brain, master of the Mercurial attributes of speech, writing, and logical, linear thinking processes. With his left hand, ruled by the right hemisphere of the brain, which supports intuitive and creative processes, he holds a lantern, lighting the way to healing states of consciousness and spiritual evolution.

Such a wise one will do the work it takes to open the swinging door between the conscious, waking mind and subconscious, dreaming mind. From within the subtle state of contemplation, the sage knows how to tap into inner stillness and shine his innermost light on peaks of aspiration and the know-how needed to live a meaningful life.

The Hermit is a sign that it's time to cultivate the best course of action and have confidence in your ability to reap a harvest for your efforts. Not surprisingly, incorrect choices can lead to difficulties and detours. Yet, the greatest wisdom comes from facing changes you weren't expecting to consider. Instead of worrying about what the future may bring, take off your shoes and feel Mother Nature's healing energy under your feet. Paying attention to your connection with the earth can inspire the wisdom within to know the steps needed for taking good care of your body and creating mental and emotional well-being.

Keywords for The Hermit

The Self
Contemplation, a wise person, reaping your harvest, shining your inner light, the fruits of self-knowledge, reaping benefits from being of service

The Shadow
Being too critical, uncertainty about outcomes, ignoring inner callings, the need for change, paying attention to healthful eating

Stirring the Mystic Cauldron

When Divining, These Align with The Hermit
The sun sign: Virgo
The rune: Ger
The archetype: The sage

Qualities They Share
Analyzing, finances, harvest, wisdom

10. The Wheel of Fortune
Also called Fortuna and Wyrd

The wheel—an age-old symbol for the up-and-down circling of life's evolving and revolving fortunes—goes round and round throughout cosmic time and space. It travels the ascending/descending, continuous momentum of expansive cycles of birth, death, repose, and rebirth. Esoterically, its nonmoving center, where all spokes on the wheel meet, is the still and silent abode of the all-seeing eye of the Great Cosmic Spirit.

Although it's common for this card to signify the turning of the wheel of fate, in this arcana's image it takes a different spin. An innocent pixie who is looking at the world with wide, all-knowing eyes tightly holds the dice of chance and change. Her glance, full of magic, mischief, and mystery, invites you to throw your dice. Will Fortuna, the goddess of luck, be with or against you?

Ultimately the toss (or the spin of the wheel) must land. Wherever it stops becomes destiny's springboard, where your sense of direction accelerates and your inner explorer comes face to face with your true self. The secrets hidden within the psyche become visible. Greater awareness emerges from having a glimpse into your inner depths, and change becomes inevitable. Tied to the beneficent and generous nature of the rune Wynn and influences of Jupiter, this card signifies that you have a good chance for winning the luck of the draw and encountering positive forces such as fruitfulness, progress, success, and financial rewards.

Keywords for The Wheel of Fortune

The Self
Prosperity, good luck, improvement, gaining momentum, the dawning of a brighter reality, progress, developing opportunities

The Shadow
Untimely transitions, a time to redefine goals, progress slowed, uncertainty about direction, gambling issues

Stirring the Mystic Cauldron

When Divining, These Align with The Wheel of Fortune
The planet: Jupiter
The rune: Wynn
The archetype: The explorer

Qualities They Share
Expansion, foresight, positivity, winning

11. Justice
Also called Adjustment

A raven, representing Lady Justice, symbol for the sign Libra and its scales of measurement, sits with firm footing on a branch blowing in the wind that dangles two equally distanced leaves. A totem of keen insight and wisdom, this sign of impartiality exists in perfect balance, able to weigh the pros and cons, the merits and demerits connected with life's joy and misery, trials and tribulations. As the feathered diplomat sits midway on her perch, she signifies the equilibrium between active and passive waves of emotions, the common denominator that weighs and balances possibilities for actions and reactions.

With outstretched wings exposing an open heart, the bird looks heavenward, seeming to seek guidance from the wind and determine how to protect her freedom with the double-edged sword of discrimination on her chest. As its point faces the earth, it appears ready to cut truth from worldly falsehoods and protect the bonds of love, partnerships, legal commitments, and processes of arbitration.

The pillars between which this female magistrate sits are black and white, representing the forces of duality, Jachin and Boaz, day-night, sun-moon, male-female, and the yes-no state of mind. The message she carries speaks to the importance of taking the middle path and choosing inner balance and even-mindedness, especially over angst and indecisiveness. When ideas struggle with juggling complex feelings, instead of pushing and pulling logical versus intuitive decisions, attentively listen to your truth with the wisdom in your heart.

Keywords for Justice

The Self
Weighing pros and cons, marriage, partnerships, finding love, cooperative actions, harmony over discord, victory, legal justice

The Shadow
Frustration, difficult decisions, unfair judgments, prejudice, unharmonious relationships, testing the truth of the soul, reevaluating commitments

Stirring the Mystic Cauldron

When Divining, These Align with Justice
The sun sign: Libra
The rune: Gyfu
The archetype: The diplomat

Qualities They Share
Balance, collaboration, fairness, mediating

12. The Hanged Man
Also called the Suspended Man

A solitary figure hangs upside down from a tree, with the full moon blossoming in the distance. While hanging downward, one of the man's legs bends at the knee and crosses behind the other, setting his legs into the sign of the cross, a sign of the material world. Beneath this cross, the man's arms fold, making his elbows point outward in opposite directions and creating the shape of an inverted triangle, an indication of the descent of the divine. Perhaps this is why some associate the tree that he hangs from with the Cabalistic Tree of Life, an esoteric pathway to enlightenment.

The outline of his body symbolically portrays detachment from the burdens of materialism, victory for spiritual aspirations, and clarifying the actions necessary to regain freedom. As a rite of passage, his dangling sacrifice has the potential to transform day-to-day consciousness into awareness of a transcendent reality.

This figure is also compared to the Norse god Odin, who hung downward from the world tree, Yggdrasil, without food or water for nine days and nights. His inward communications and the suffering of the physical body were an offering to the gods. When he became exhausted and considered giving up his quest, he looked at the ground beneath him and the runic alphabet magically appeared. Surging with sparks of renewal, he reached down and swept the runes into his hands. The unexpected illumination from the letters initiated not only a sacred oracle, but also an evolutionary passage for a written language to come into life.

As an image of unrelenting austerity, this card can be viewed as the archetypal journey of the mystic. It draws attention to benefits of a meditative path or quest for transcending ordinary awareness and spiritual awakening. It signals the importance of tapping into Neptune's and Lagu's watery energy and looking at your cards and stones from a mystical point of view.

Keywords for The Hanged Man

The Self
Detaching from being "hung up," something triggers a transcendent awareness, seeking truth, sacrifice, a vision quest

The Shadow
Being hung up, not trusting your intuition, battling pressure / outward stress, challenges to face, clouded issues

Stirring the Mystic Cauldron

When Divining, These Align with The Hanged Man
The planet: Neptune
The rune: Lagu
The archetype: The mystic

Qualities They Share
Dreams, illusion, intuition, nonconformity

13. Death
Also called Rebirth and Reincarnation

Death appears as an elder with the skin and bones typically viewed on a corpse that has been parched in a desert. Her long, white hair fans out in all directions, with soaring waves of dancing shadows silently displaying her power and strength. Vibrant flowers in her hair contrast with her skin, wrinkled by the scorn of quickly passing time. As if living between the worlds, she looks out from the depths of her dark, lifeless eyes to honor her shrouded mission and let her onlookers know that she has been summoned by the invisible forces of the great beyond.

All cards have a multitude of meanings, and this one is no different. Its appearance in your spread can indicate a physical death, but don't jump to this literal interpretation, since it's not always its meaning. When viewing this image's stark composure, think further than the possibility of physical oblivion, by discussing its esoteric significance. It may refer to the death of a relationship or the end to an undertaking. It is directly linked with the sun sign Scorpio, the run Eoh, and the archetype of transformation and birth, death, and rebirth, which serves as a reminder that as one thing comes to an end, something new is about to take its place.

As the sun sets, signaling the end of a day, it is rising for others, who see it awakening the dawn. Only by mentally dying to the familiar can one experience the evolution of awareness and step out of what was, into a new hope for what might be. We cannot stop the up-and-down waves of life from flowing into the Ocean of Transformation. With death, all attachments are broken, and with rebirth, the dormant sense of self gives way to renewal. A snake sheds its skin to grow into a renewed body. Like the caterpillar shifting to become a butterfly, trust the changes that life is bringing, even if the outcome is unknown.

Keywords for the Death card

The Self
Transformation, rebirth, evolution, changing emotions, sensual energy, intuition, new resources, secrecy, psychic clarity

The Shadow
Resisting change, jealousy, emotional complexity, fear-centered, unforgiving, facing fears of death

Stirring the Mystic Cauldron

When Divining, These Align with Death
The sun sign: Scorpio
The rune: Eoh
The archetype: The phoenix

Qualltles They Share
Rebirth, transformation, the psychic, secretive

14. Temperance
Also called Art and the Alchemist

An angel is dressed in white flowing gowns, the sign for innocence, virginity, and purity. Her wings of light are outstretched majestically while she rides a white horse, a symbol for the steed of Rhiannon, Queen of Faeries and the Celtic goddess of fertility and rebirth. Both horse and rider seem to be stepping through an otherworldly mist beyond ordinary beauty. It is through moderation, one of the four virtues, that this elegant being mediates control of desires and is a glowing model of self-mastery. Her golden crown illuminates the third eye, doorway to prophecy and psychic insight.

Don't overthink your card's image for Temperance. Little by little you'll come to understand this archetypal teacher who brings understanding of how to walk the moderate, middle path between the dark and the light, the conscious and the subconscious, matter and spirit. Her ultimate destination includes a meeting at the doorway to the divine, the balancing point between the left and right hemispheres of the brain—an essential location on the mind map that points the way to empowering your creativity and intuition.

When you select this card, it's time for the contemplation of your present quest and moderating inner balance and self-control. Your inner alchemist will be finding new avenues for expanding perceptions, be they wild or tame, and you'll be gaining more understanding of how to walk the middle path, where it becomes feasible to stay calm during turbulent times.

Keywords for Temperance

The Self
Saying "No" to what you don't want and "Yes" to what you do want, finding your center, moderation, spiritual enrichment

The Shadow
Lacking temperance, the need for inner balance, going against your ideals, incompatibility with other's demands

Stirring the Mystic Cauldron

When Divining, These Align with Temperance
The sun sign: Sagittarius
The rune: Rad
The archetype: The teacher

Qualities They Share
Optimism, philosophy, expansive, travel

15. The Devil
Also called the Black Magician and Lord of Matter

The ancient Lord of Hades, whom religion has given the names Satan, Lucifer, and Beelzebub, appears on this card as a Pan-like god with long, goat-shaped horns curving downward. He sits like of a bird of prey, looking down at an innocent child who seems to be contemplating earthly matters. A dark figure covered in shadows, this archetype of authority and mischievous deeds gives a sense of impending chaos, even though a pyramid, a sign of wisdom, wealth, and power, rises in the nearby distance.

Fearsome as The Devil may be, when he appears in your card spread, it doesn't necessarily mean something bad is going to happen. It might represent something unpleasant, or it might not. When you're reading for a querent, it's important to focus on this card's myriad possible interpretations in order to avoid creating anxiety that may or may not be warranted. Even if the devil is known as the prince of darkness, alternative interpretations include connections with the archetype of authority, or the pagan god Pan's celebration of the joys of sensuality, staying alert to negative thinking, and not becoming attached to hedonistic desires.

If you talk about the devil in the conventional Christian view of good and evil, he is God's beloved fallen angel who claims the position of the leading authority on manipulation and temptation. His power is in his name, which conjures fear and thoughts of facing a downward tumble.

As such, this card can indicate a confrontation with the shadow side of one's personality or any challenge that restricts, upsets, or frustrates positive efforts, including sexual traumas or dysfunctions. It can also be a warning to remove chains of oppression, manipulation, or negativity that dam feelings of well-being. Or, it can be a message to run from the authority who points you in a direction that doesn't feel like your true path. If you feel that this card represents living in a heartless hell, you might question whose responsibility it is to change those conditions, and redouble your efforts to bring about a change to create opportunities for finding peace of mind.

Keywords for The Devil

The Self
A challenge, a difficult emotional situation, being chained to an inharmonious situation, losing sight of priorities, focusing on limits

The Shadow
Anxiety shadows hopes, unjust restrictions, dealing with financial or romantic chaos, something's wrong but you can't sort it out

Stirring the Mystic Cauldron

When Divining, These Align with The Devil
The sun sign: Capricorn
The rune: Nyd
The archetype: The authority

Qualities They Share
Finances, focus, responsibility, maturity

16. The Tower
Also called the House of God

The crashing tower, sometimes referred to as the Tower of Babel, has a castle-in-the-air, dreamlike appearance. As it falls, a beautiful woman, tethered to it by chains, reaches toward the heavens, struggling to overcome her undesirable fate. A royal crown, the symbol of power, control, and achievement, falls from the woman's head as she confronts the forces of destruction that are exploding beyond her command. We can only hope that she survives the multiple thunderbolts dropping down in a dark, violent rage, and that she wins her struggle against a descending ruin.

The outcome of the falling tower can be compared to an overactive, fiery aspect of Mars, and the volatile nature of being caught in the vaporous fumes of transformation. But even if events may unexpectedly shake someone to their core, counting blessings can increase good feelings in spite of a crumbling belfry. Welcomed or not, facing change can ignite our hunger to succeed without fear of falling from the enchanting towers of our dreams.

When temporal structures built on foundations of worldly desires begin to collapse, it's a strong statement that something needs to change. With acceptance or not, it's time for reassessment of one's reality, especially if it includes being locked within a turret of toiling demands. Unexpected life circumstances may be shocking, but they can also be the perfect excuse to realign and redesign a more realistic vision of your best self. With the dissolution of the tower comes the opportunity for structuring a new pathway to uplift your spirits and give hope for a brighter future. Even if there are times when we must battle conflict in life, our way of dealing with a "crumbling tower" can make it a curse or turn it into a blessing.

Keywords for The Tower

The Self
Competition, anger, out-of-control emotions, disruption of plans, growing tension, focusing to protect your interests

The Shadow
An unexpected crisis, accidents, sexual tensions, panic, vulnerabilities are exposed, panic, a shaking foundation

Stirring the Mystic Cauldron

When Divining, These Align with The Tower
The planet: Mars
The rune: Feoh
The archetype: The initiator

Qualities They Share
Action, confrontation, competition, autonomy

17. The Star
Also called Illumination and Dog Star

In this card's image, with a lustrous glow visible only in the dark, the stars shine bright for the benefit of all, whether prince or pauper. In Egyptian mythology, the canopy of the stars was associated with the goddess Nuit, a beautiful cosmic woman visible in the nighttime sky, covered by countless stars. Esoterically, she was respected as the knower of all things, who possessed the unimaginable brilliance of celestial light shining through every corner of the universe.

In the ubiquitous Pamela Colman Smith card image in the Rider-Waite Tarot, the freedom-loving archetype represented by The Star is portrayed as a naked maiden. Her one knee rests upon solid ground, a sign of having an unshakable, earthly foundation. Her right foot floats motionless on the surface of a reflecting pool filled with the water of life that mirrors the depth in the subconscious, letting us know that her spiritual heredity is not bound by the rules of the material world. With an intuitive power capable of delving into realities beyond those discerned by the five senses, she effortlessly balances the subtle and the gross, the light and the dark, and the inner and outer self.

A humble representative of the spirited sun sign Aquarius and the rune Mann, this star is linked with illumination, clarity of purpose, and the pursuit of a peaceful world. Esoterically it is said to alleviate ignorance, doubts, or confusion, and to reform, enlighten, and guide one to seeing the inner light. The Star also invokes an invisible power that brightens one's soul-self with an awe-inspiring healing of painful issues.

Keywords for The Star

The Self
Positive energy, visions for improvement, clarity, intuitive insights, heightened awareness, inner revolution, evolutionary ideas

The Shadow
Misunderstandings, lack of clarity or goals, confusing ideals with reality, a need to brighten one's attitude

Stirring the Mystic Cauldron

When Divining, These Align with The Star
The sun sign: Aquarius
The rune: Mann
The archetype: The reformer

Qualities They Share
Humanitarian, upbeat, empathy, freedom

18. The Moon
Also called Luna

The moon shines its guiding light in the dark of night on the path to inner evolution. In this card, its face is the shining image of Hathor, the ancient Egyptian mother goddess of the sky, beauty, music, dancing, and intuition, who was worshiped to protect the home and family. She boldly shoots arrows at the sun to encourage its brilliance to call forth the day and warm the earth. Her vulture mask is a sign of her power to see beyond external reality and into the watery depths of the psyche, where the ultimate journey to align emotions can be witnessed. Throughout time, the moon has been tied to nurturing the inner spirit, feminine mysteries, the menstrual cycle, childbirth, emotions, domesticity, the imagination, dreams, memories, and esoterica. Its energy flows in the womb to water the seeds of life and signals undercurrents in the senses to connect with instinctual, gut feelings.

While constantly moving through its different phases, the moon voices its silence by reflecting the light of the sun and mirroring the inner wisdom of the higher self. Crawling like elusive crustaceans outward from the protective harbors of the subconscious mind, its shadowy reflections sometimes emerge to illuminate some hidden aspect of the mind, such as unconscious emotional blocks or wounds buried in the past. Our willingness to face what lies buried deep within can inspire a healing alignment with the truth, within which worries disappear in waves of renewed acceptance and peace of mind.

Over time, watching the changing lunar phases and noting one's inner reactions to them can help strengthen our trust in our instinctive knowing, which is comparable to an owl's ability to see in the dark.

Keywords for The Moon

The Self
Imagination, empathy, intense emotions, making heart connections, potential change, home improvements, memories stir

The Shadow
Waning energy, taking an emotional dive, changes create worry, deception, uncertainties about direction, illusion

Stirring the Mystic Cauldron

When Divining, These Align with The Moon
The sun sign: Pisces
The rune: Hoegl
The archetype: The intuitive

Qualities They Share
Instinct, understanding, imagination, caring

19. The Sun
Also called Awakening and Lord of Fire

A brilliant sun setting over a wide, barren desert portrays a moment of soul-searching stillness. Sending its golden rays racing across the sky, it illuminates a path to joy, growth, healing, and regeneration. A solo traveler rides a camel, the ancient Egyptian symbol of wealth, trust, and endurance, and treks toward the endless horizon. High above, the sky displays the silent motion of planetary cycles.

The card entwined with this life-giving orb shares its glow with the archetype of the self and its unifying awareness of mind, body, and emotions. It can indicate a pilgrimage into the furthest reaches of your conscious mind, where you may find the qualities that make you who you are. Unless negative forces make the heat of the sun excessive, it naturally shines a beneficial light over any concerns you or your client might have. It inspires the attitude of a winner and brings clarity to answer questions that until now may have been hidden from view.

The sun shines on self-reliance, free will, creative self-expression, happiness, and a positive disposition. Worshiped in ancient Egypt as the god Ra, guardian of the light of day, the sky, and the earth beneath it, the sun is associated with vibrant energy, fertility, and fruitfulness of life. Its light offers a warm glow and nourishment that energizes the sprouting seeds of the life and empowers the will to rise from bed in the morning.

Keywords for The Sun

The Self
Joy, victory, the unleashing of creative forces, dynamic self-expression, masculine or yang energy, personal empowerment, healing

The Shadow
Too much drying heat, lacking energy, the need to heal the body or emotions, not enough laughter, experiencing creative blocks

Stirring the Mystic Cauldron

When Divining, These Align with The Sun
The planet: The sun
The rune: Sigel
The archetype: The self

Qualities They Share
Vitality, creativity, children, happiness

20. Judgement
Also called the Angel and the Aeon

At the final destination of their journey, a naked man and woman ascend from open coffins. Hoping for good news as to what's coming next, they lift their arms toward archangel Gabriel, who sits on a cloud with his wings expanded across the luminous sky. Blowing his celestial trumpet, he looks knowingly toward the mortals, who are listening to his call for truth. Embodying heavenly notes, its magical sound initiates a soulful peace, release from attachments, and the destruction of desire's demands.

Associated with the celebration of life and archetypal rebirth, this card typifies the vast potentials of renewal and revival in body, mind, emotions, and spirit. In a card spread, only the cards surrounding Judgement can highlight what type of renewal is being called forth. Transitions may include liberation from past pain, getting off an unpleasant ride on a merry-go-round of regret or guilt, or the completion of an ongoing cycle of pain or blame. Oppositely, it can indicate an uplifting change of attitude or a renewed sense of purpose. Only upward energy comes from gathering the courage to face mistakes knowingly or unknowing made, no matter how scary or dark they may be.

Because this card is associated with Pluto, the instigator of changing perceptions, the understanding of its underlying significance can sometimes jolt one's core. Questions involving the judgment of emotions may not be answered without triggering a sense of unfairness and an avalanche of defensive response. One can hope that the untamed nature both of helpful and scouring judgments can be experienced with a warning sign encouraging beneficial soul-brightening realignment.

Keywords for Judgement

The Self
Changing realities, third eye, nonverbal perceptions, altered plans, finding a new calling, generational judgment on another generation

The Shadow
Uncertainty, questioning self-worth, rehashing old criticism, harsh judgments, guilt, experiencing the whip of judgment

Stirring the Mystic Cauldron

When Divining, These Align with Judgement
The planet: Pluto
The rune: Ing
The archetype: Rebirth

Qualities They Share
Transformation, disruption, the subconscious, mystery

21. The World
Also called Universe, the Cosmos, or Prudence

Untainted by mortal ignorance, the Greek goddess Sophia stands in the center of a laurel wreath, a sign of victory, unity, wholeness, and completion. As a universal Mother, (although some claim this figure to be androgynous), her unequaled power to be queen of the world transcends the need of a worldly throne, for she knows that her love showers light and love on all, be they royal or downtrodden.

Expressing joy, her naked figure demonstrates the freedom to live without shame, guilt, or fear of society's constraints and condemnations. Her mythic might ignites flames over her heart, illuminating the virtues of prudence, faith, hope, and charity. With the know-how to balance the fire, earth, air, and water elements, she sprouts seeds in her sacred garden through miracles, awe, and wonder. Through her openness to the world, she shares qualities with the archetypal wise elder, who avows that the powers of concentration, discipline, and hard work can free the mind from tethers of fear, doubt, or insecurity. Her warmhearted stance gives credence to the Saturnian sense that a giving hand is stronger than one that selfishly takes.

A sign of faith in worldly opportunities, this card is a reminder to use your strengths and skills to set intentions to live a prosperous life. As the last of the Major Arcana cards, it suggests that the trials of life can be won. Rewards for past efforts are due; the novice has arrived at the finish line on the path to becoming the adept.

Keywords for The World

The Self
Maturity, knowing the self, completion, wisdom is won through experience, selfless love, initiation, finding answers, worldliness

The Shadow
Setting boundaries, relearning old lessons, recognizing past patterns, self-doubt, insecurities, time challenges

Stirring the Mystic Cauldron

When Divining, These Align with The World
The planet: Saturn
The rune: Peordh
The archetype: The wise elder

Qualities They Share
Karma, values, responsibility, limits

0. The Fool
Also called the Jester and the Vagabond

THE FOOL 00

The Fool, often depicted as a free-spirited youth, stumbles between yin-feminine-lunar and yang-masculine-solar forces while walking along the edge of a cliff. Wearing a jester's cap, he (or is it a she?) appears to be oblivious to where he is going, while a small dog barks at his heels, warning him of a potentially dangerous fall. This bold, archetypal child lives in awe of life's many splendors, acting spontaneously in a joyful oneness with each moment. Living in the present while playfully following his instincts, he juggles the lessons of the past with a detached fearlessness of what the future will bring. Ignoring society's advice to work hard and make lots of money, The Fool has no desire to conform to others' expectations.

Sometimes compared with the Roman god Bacchus and Dionysus, the Greek god of wine, pleasure, and wild abandon, this Fool is certainly not foolish. He is the adept who has transcended the concerns of the material world and the need for society's approval. His card is numbered zero, a number without boundaries that holds the sole honor of balancing between alpha, the first, and omega, the last major card.

Living without material possessions, The Fool detaches from others' conceptions of how to live. Searching for the guiding star of enlightenment, he listens to the songs of etheric sirens and the peerless poetry of celestial muses. While being lifted ever upward by lithe winds to dance in waves of vibrational light, he invites us to join his journey. Finding wholeness and balancing our inclinations to be tethered versus being free of worldly desires is one step forward in knowing how not to stumble when walking alongside this wise fool.

Keywords for The Fool

The Self

Innocence, the pursuit of being free spirited, an unexpected adventure, living in the now, freedom-loving, nonconforming values

The Shadow

Hindrance of one's personal freedom, refusing to accept society's demands, the need to listen to one's inner child

Stirring the Mystic Cauldron

When Divining, These Align with The Fool

The planet: Uranus
The rune: Daeg
The archetype: The child

Qualities They Share

The unexpected, freedom, innovation, unrest

CHAPTER 8

TWENTY-FOUR SECRETS CHISELED IN STONE

Newsworthy Notes

The time you spend playing with your runes helps you build a personal connection with each stone. Using the term "stone" does not ignore the momentum they've gathered over thousands of years, with people using them to look at life through oracular eyes.

To truly have a personal relationship with the runes, you need to investigate their various symbols in terms of what they mean to you. When you are familiar with the zodiac and know the rune-astrological correlations, you have a fantastic tool to unlock their meanings and mysteries.

Aligning Runes with Astrological Keys

When divining, you can hope to connect intuitively with the runes, but when first learning to work with them, it's useful to call upon their astrological connections to gain understanding of their core qualities. Despite the wise tracing their meanings to the fabled world of their early beginnings, many scholars present insightful and worthwhile revelations in relation to their astrological correlations.

My correlations are influenced by my initial teachers many decades ago. I was first introduced to runes by Ralph Blum and Deon Dolphin, both longtime rune casters. My humble thanks to both of these remarkable teachers, who spent their life sharing their ideas and rune writings before passing to the other side.

Keyword Meanings

You'll find upright rune meanings listed under the keyword heading titled "The Self." Reversed rune meanings are listed under the keyword heading "The Shadow."

A general rule: If a rune is neither upright nor reversed, read it as upright or reversed, depending on the degree of the slant of a symbol after it falls on your table. If it is only slightly slanted downward, its interpretations should be discussed mostly as an upright stone. If a symbol slants mostly downward, it can be read using more of its shadow interpretations.

Because interpretations for the stones are influenced by the cultural backgrounds of the people citing them, an open mind is a valuable asset when you are learning about them. Think about creating your own keyword list of their attributes when and if you're reading different modern rune authors. In time, your list can evolve to help you assess and integrate their central meanings into your practice.

Daeg and Ethel

You may notice that the twenty-third and twenty-fourth runes are in a disputed order. The scholarly controversy concerning the placement of Daeg and Ethel and which rune comes before or after the other is not resolved. Both systems are in current use.

The Blank Rune

There aren't any records of the ancients using a blank stone. Also called the Rune of Wyrd (fate), it is used by some modern rune casters but not by others, who follow the ancient ways. It's up to you if you include a blank stone with your set or not. For those who keep a blank stone in their bag, its meanings can include the following: the answer to a question is unknowable, it's the wrong time to ask your question, let your intuition fill in the blank, or it isn't the right time to ask your question.

TOUCHING THE SPIRIT IN THE RUNES

1. Feoh
English translation: cattle, money

Feoh is the first letter in the elder futhark. It signifies finding the courage to step into action and turn ideas into greater opportunities. Aligned with powerful Mars energy, it enlightens the initial sparks of courage to act and the determination to prosper. Because it takes more than going ice fishing to survive the freezing-cold northern winters, this rune reminds one to take extra measures to stay warm and tend the hearth. In bygone times, Feoh would be a reminder to tap into the protective matrix of boundless energy of the Aesir gods, to honor them with sacrifice, and to work hard and sharpen the cutting edge of their blades. One must be ready to fight the merciless giants who might unexpectedly come to destroy their hope for survival by claiming their resources and life-giving provisions.

Also, Feoh was a sign for material wealth such as cattle or weapons. With such tangible property also came the power to influence others. A family who owned cattle had prestige and the ability to pay debts. Such a person could even buy passage out of difficulties and better navigate complex situations.

Feoh's archetype, the initiator, echoes the modern value of stepping up and confidently using your talents to do something of value for the herd. Once interpreted as a "fee" or energy exchange, Feoh can assume different usages as long as it includes living with passion as the starring role in one's efforts. Confidence is required to combat the mundane and the pressures of stress, but when one is bold enough to assert their will, this stone is auspicious for taking leading actions and winning over challenging circumstances.

Keywords for Feoh

The Self
Forceful persuasion, positive, fiery energy, good finances, adopting a winning attitude, leading the way, gaining confidence

The Shadow
Wanting power, the need to move forward, frustrations in relation to beginning new projects, facing debt, financial woes

Stirring the Mystic Cauldron

When Divining, These Align with Feoh
The planet: Mars
The card: The Tower
The archetype: The initiator

Qualities They Share
Action, confrontation, competition, autonomy

2. Ur
English translation: aurochs or wild oxen

To the Teutons, mighty Ur was one with the invisible strength of the archetypal shaman, healer, and guide in this and other worlds. In the old Norse myth of creation, it was associated with Audhumla, the ice-licking cow with horns like a bull, who was considered to be the mother of the universe and sustainer of the world. From the licking of her tongue came forth the Aesir gods, who fathered the human race. As a creative, godlike force, Ur stood for the uncommon power to look through the third eye, give birth to new creations, and manifest joyful miracles in a realm bound by the restraints of cold weather, frequent wars, and hardship.

In current times, comparable to the zodiac earth sign of the bull that yields strength and power, Ur is a sign of the hidden potential to jump forth with determination to persist and overcome the challenges of uncertainty. Hold this rune in your hand when you need healing or are being pushed to go beyond limitations, and affirm your healthy, physical body. Ur is the call to break ties with suppressing doubts or inhibiting fears and to own your power to connect with the depth of wisdom within your being and transform any conflict into discovery.

It can also be a sign to spend time in nature and bind your energy with the earth to expand your sense of your inner space. As did the ancients, you can call on the power of Ur to charge your inner spirit with the courage to move seamlessly toward your greater good and smell the flowers along your way.

Keywords for Ur

The Self
Rebirth of awareness, stimulating creative potentials, financial or emotional beneficial insights, determination fuels opportunities to advance

The Shadow
Broken dreams, confusion, not following your gut instinct, ignoring potential opportunities, conflict of interest, dissatisfaction

Stirring the Mystic Cauldron

When Divining, These Align with Ur
The sun sign: Taurus
The card: The High Priest
The archetype: The shaman

Qualities They Share
Determination, fertility, stability, affection

3. Thorn English translation: thorn

In ancient Germanic societies, Thorn indicated confrontation with the forces of destruction. It cautioned the unmistaken need for protection from the difficulties that challenged survival. A red flag, it warned of foes such as the ice giants, who sent howling blizzards to diminish food supplies, or the mischievous elves, dwarfs, trolls, or any other unearthly creature who could decrease the life-giving forces of all-providing Mother Nature.

Thorn was a sign that there could be a curse against you, and the resulting need to invoke Frigg, Odin's wife and supreme goddess, to rise above the challenges that could impede progress or interfere with one's well-being, home, and emotional security. Or perhaps the archetypal maiden would need to be summoned from her resting state to rise and bless an amulet made to confront the waves of perplexing toil that could prevent successful gathering and hunting.

For modern rune sleuths, the appearance of this rune can indicate a test of emotional intelligence that forces one to overcome limitations and reassess values. If you're dealing with thorny issues, it's time to release their hold on you, fortify your primary efforts, and shield your sensitivities to strengthen your will to overcome negativities. It's also good to remember that when a circumstance is viewed as a personal disaster, it can often turn out to be a blessing in disguise. The waves in the ocean of life are always flowing back and forth, and trouble can turn to triumph in a short amount of time.

Keywords for Thorn

The Self
Disruption, uncertainty, challenges create anxiety, "thorny" issues, fortify your outlook and a positive attitude, listen to your intuition

The Shadow
Inner tensions, possible violence, the need to summon your inner warrior for psychic self-defense, reassure overly sensitive emotions

Stirring the Mystic Cauldron

When Divining, These Align with Thorn
The planet: The waning moon
The card: The High Priestess
The archetype: The maiden

Qualities They Share
Challenge, oppression, taboo, travel

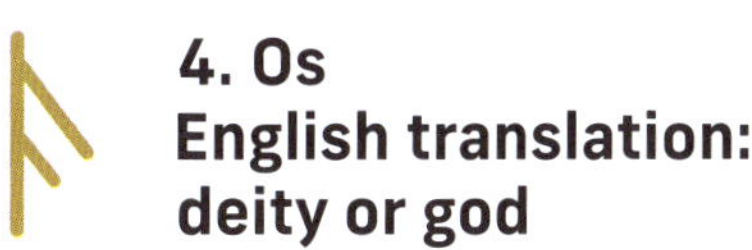

4. Os
English translation: deity or god

In days of yore, whoever possessed the command of spoken words could assume a power over others that not many could obtain, and be allowed special advantages among their clan. Even more amazing were the special times when one could channel inspirational messages from signs found in nature, talk with the spirits of the ancestors, and express a visionary wisdom to guide destiny. When Os—equal to the breath of life, fire of the mind, and the power to heal—was drawn, it was a magical sign foretelling that the will of God was being echoed through human words. It was so powerful that it assumed a special place of honor in rhyme, song, and myth.

In current times, Os—the archetype of healing and inspirational communications—is a sign of the importance of owning your personal magic, expressing the power of your ideas, and aligning your actions with your spoken words. It points to listening to the intuitive voice bubbling in the cauldron of your mind that arises from your direct experience with untamed forces in the depth of your psyche.

Comparable to Mercurial qualities such as communication, curiosity, and travel, this rune silently verbalizes that you can expect a letter, email, or phone call to deliver a message of importance. You might receive news concerning the physical or financial world that may increase your certainty about your direction. It can also indicate new possibilities for the joyful springing forth of your emotional or spiritual unfoldment. You may divine the unknown, increase intuitive awareness, or find a focus that enhances your sense of purpose. Mostly auspicious, it's a reminder to honor your birthright to drink from the healing well of the sublime—or maybe have a cup of mead.

Keywords for Os

The Self
Clarity, sprouting new ideas, strength in communication, enthusiasm, getting information or important messages, healing

The Shadow
Faulty logic, manipulation, insecurities concerning health, nervous energy, lack of clarity, misinformation, or unresolved closure

Stirring the Mystic Cauldron

When Divining, These Align With Os
The planet: Mercury
The card: The Magician
The archetype: The healer

Qualities They Share
Communication, travel, youthfulness, magic

5. Rad
English translation: journey

To the ancients, Rad, a sign of expansiveness and exploration, was associated with adventure, riding, motion, travel, and long journeys. Even if pathways were not friendly, and maps nonexistent, each brave wanderer could call upon this rune to safely guide his or her way across the unknown waters of their destiny. For some, this sign might represent fulfilling the dream of the journey across the rainbow bridge. Even if one couldn't join Thor riding his chariot across the sky, with the sign Rad nearby he or she could divine the higher meaning of one's destination through its message.

A sign of movement and transport, its mark indicates either inward or external actions for worldly or spiritual gain. Events to stimulate new awareness, searching the world for higher philosophies, and summoning the spirit of the quest are qualities metaphorically pointing to the true north of its extended reach. It was chiseled to honor the essential nature of one's individuality yet inspired the strength to embrace tribal unity.

Rad is comparable to an archetypal teacher, guru, mentor, or coach who transports you to higher levels of understanding and increases clarity about your place in the cosmos. Wearing it as your talisman, you may awaken to hear a voice that echoes a message that you're in reach of the fullness of life and love. The momentum of your passage through the maze of understanding mind and emotion, will, and passion moves quickly forward under Rad's fountain of free-flowing knowledge. Ride its vibrational currents to gather insights to know beyond any doubt what steps need to be taken to arrive at your desired destination.

Keywords for Rad

The Self
Protection, travel, intellectual insights, making choices, taking action, moving in a timely fashion, finding direction, fulfilling ambitions

The Shadow
Lack of perceptivity, insincerity, becoming drained by circumstance, altered or frustrated travel plans

Stirring the Mystic Cauldron

When Divining, These Align with Rad
The sun sign: Sagittarius
The card: Temperance
The archetype: The teacher

Qualities They Share
Optimism, philosophy, expansion, travel

6. Cen
English translation: torch

To ease the pain of life's uncertainties, it was natural to seek the peace of the forest and call on Mother Nature for her grace to become one with the wisdom of Cen, the rune of blazing insights, inspiration, and transformation. As an archetype, this rune arouses the hope for the magic of miracles to ignite the torch of soul knowledge. It embodies the enchanting glow of a dancing flame in the dark corners of consciousness that vanquishes fear of the unknown and daunting ghosts of ignorance.

To the ancients, Cen was equal to a power that could scare off wild beasts in the night and ignite the bonfires of their hope and hearths, the main source of warmth and protection from the chill of harsh winds. It is connected with the Norse goddess of the sun, Sol, who, in her ceremonial robes of alluring enchantment, sang charmed songs to chase away the long, dark winter nights. Also, some call this Loki's rune of illumination—he was the dualistic god of mischief and greatness—and the power of the sixth sense.

Cen represents a regenerative power that can heal perceptions and set one free from misery. A sign of the kindling of friendship and the sparks of creativity, it enlightens good instincts for finding circles of protection, successful trading of goods, and knowing one's best direction.

Keywords for Cen

The Self
Inner light, clarity, a torch of strength, the courage to face obstacles, overcoming anxiety, finding happiness, creativity, healing

The Shadow
Confidence needs rebuilding, darkness overshadowing light, creative goals need stronger effort, fiery emotions

Stirring the Mystic Cauldron

When Divining, These Align with Cen
The sun sign: Leo
The card: Strength
The archetype: The enchanter

Qualities They Share
Vitality, boldness, heroism, happiness

7. Gyfu English translation: gifts

A glyph with two lines of equal length that cross to make the sign of an x, Gyfu marks the spot where the power of two forces equally comes together. It communicates the importance of maintaining a positive outlook and trusting that one's intuition will result in receiving a helpful message from the gods. It can be a sign that gifts could arrive in the form of talents or skills that could improve one's chances for success. To the Norse, this symbol represented the delicate balance of influences that could encourage a mutual give-and-take relationship such as a marriage or hunting-and-gathering collective that would increase the chances for positive outcomes and peaceful communities.

In olden times, communication with Spirit was a sacred yet practical reality as essential as the breath of life. People who could communicate with the magic in nature were the archetypal diplomats who could tune into the rhythms of the seasons, negotiate and harmonize imbalances within the clan, and declare the correct lunar timing to celebrate life's passages with song, sacrifice, ritual, and uplifting incantations.

When interpreting the meaning of Gyfu, consider what purpose two separate, distinct energies or two paths have for coming together. What gifts will result from two forces merging or when two separate influences unite? If two people cross each other's paths, such as the child and the parent, the hostess and the guest, the teacher and the student, the lover and the beloved, or other manifestations of individual energies coming together, how might they come into play in the right phase of your or your client's life, and what gifts or opportunities might they bring?

Keywords for Gyfu

The Self
The crossing of two paths, two energies merging, two forces coming together, beneficial relationships, magic meets reason, gifts

The Shadow
Being forced to meet in the middle when you're not ready, expectations not being met, imbalance, the push and pull of duality

Stirring the Mystic Cauldron

When Divining, These Align with Gyfu
The sun sign: Libra
The card: Justice
The archetype: The diplomat

Qualities They Share
Balance, collaboration, fairness, mediating

8. Wynn English translation: joy

Wynn is the sign of joy, glory, and positive experiences. For the ancients, whose lives were often filled with struggles of survival and the panic of war, happy times were celebrated by the pouring of mead, the delight of song, and the poetry or storytelling recited by the bard, which filled the air with the spirit of merriment. Its inspirational magic could arouse hopes of glories yet to be experienced. Its presence could lessen fears of gruesome giants and the day of evil's reckoning, called Ragnarokk, when doom would bring an end to the world of the Aesir gods (interpreted by some as the time when Christians denied pagans their rights to use the runes or to worship their ancient gods).

Auspicious, this rune highlights good health, an uplifted sense of well-being, and moving toward a winning direction. Its zodiacal ties with Jupiter link it with optimism and the archetype of the explorer who seeks to discover possibilities for an expansive view both of the horizon and the heavens. Like a neon sign, it might be telling you to take the time to connect with your social tribe and create opportunities for good times or social brainstorming to find creative resolutions to problems. After all, when this rune drops from your pouch, it bodes well for knowing what steps you need to journey toward prosperity. Wynn is like a shining mirror that reflects the wisdom within. It is a signal to trust that your ideas will conquer life's challenges and improve your chances for winning. The cup of mead is always half full, not half empty.

Keywords for Wynn

The Self
Joy, pleasure; finding resolutions to problems; improving circumstance; healing the body, mind, and spirit; serendipity; winning

The Shadow
Losing investments of time or money, an adventure is postponed or canceled, ignoring your own wisdom, overindulgence

Stirring the Mystic Cauldron

When Divining, These Align with Wynn
The planet: Jupiter
The card: Wheel of Fortune
The archetype: The explorer

Qualities They Share
Expansion, foresight, positivity, winning

9. Hoegl
English translation: hail

Chanting to the gods, dancing ecstatically, and igniting sacred fires were undertaken to soothe the uncontrollable, icy forces of nature sent by the winter gods. For the Teutons, Hoegl equaled hail and the undisputed rights of nature. When divined, it forewarned that the gods must be appeased. What might the clan do to honor their gods, yet push back on nature and the threat that hail could bring? To face the worrisome potentials that they feared, they would often seek insight from the Volva or seer and request helpful messages from the voice of the oracle. Would they be safe rowing across the water of life when frozen droplets of ice descended from the flurry of the sky gods?

However, one could gain understanding of the future, when hail would fall into a pool of water and stir the reflecting light of the moon in its depth. It also increased the potency of movements in the ocean of the emotions and the fluctuating tides of self-reflection. Also, frozen memories holding hostage over the head and heart might be warmed with its message to honor the god of the frost with prayerful reverie.

Hoegl, the ruler of the second aettir, can be the silent voice of your intuition telling you to prepare for changes that may shake stability. Expectations of what "should be" may need to be left behind if one holds too tightly to heart's unrealistic desires. You may give or get the cold shoulder, emotions may seem hard to control, and decision-making may be as easy as catching a fish out of water. Just as hail melts quickly, it does not necessarily mean a long-term crisis, but it is a sign to be extra attentive in caring for your needs now and in the nearby future. If you stay centered in your instincts, you may notice that Hoegl brings an opportunity to meet the intuitive archetype and hear whisperings that awaken emotional understanding.

Keywords for Hoegl

The Self
An intuitive sensing, strong moods and emotions, the need to be centered and grounded, patience is needed to resolve issues

The Shadow
Setbacks, confusion, vulnerability—either emotionally or psychically, the need to fortify your space with loving kindness

Stirring the Mystic Cauldron

When Divining, These Align with Hoegl
The sun sign: Pisces
The card: The Moon
The archetype: The intuitive

Qualities They Share
Instinct, understanding, imagination, caring

10. Nyd English translation: need, despair

Nyd is connected with the archetypal authority of those such as the Fates, who, in olden times, were personified as three very old women who wove threads of many colors on a loom entwining human destiny. These mystical beings would often contact the forces of delay, limitation, or turmoil and bring upset to disturb one's sense of having authority over his or her own life. Unfortunately, the discordant meaning linked with this rune was too easily grasped by the ancients, whose struggles could be desperately grim, and facing death was just as common as surviving the spoils of war's victory. Even the beneficent gods wouldn't always stop villages from being plundered and clansmen from being slain.

For modern rune casters, Nyd may be read with a bit lighter meaning than its potential somber message, and it can be invoked to inspire spirited musings that underlie the determination to win the myriad battles of life. At its best, Nyd is a signal to summon your strength to flow with the struggles that the seasons may bring, and turn your pain into gain. In its favor, it can indicate the coming time of personal growth through hardships that force you to move faster toward a sense of winning over challenges.

Whether Nyd equals the need for resources depends on one's willingness to persevere through difficulties and to take responsibility for finding what is required to overcome fears about what is next to come. Perhaps it is Loki, the Norse trickster god, who is demanding that we summon our earthly strength and persistence to face complexities and empower our inner warrior. Often portrayed as a force to overcome, it conveys the need to act cautiously, patiently, and judiciously, while highlighting the importance of harnessing one's power to transform frustrations into opportunities for growth, discovery, and success. Staying warmhearted, even when it's cold outside, may benefit both your watery emotional and earthly financial needs. This is especially true if you are pursuing ideas that strengthen your inner structure and support your efforts to become the master of your fate.

Keywords for Nyd

The Self
A need to fulfill, a challenge to overcome, a serious situation, limitations, the testing of values, the need to focus, finding resolutions

The Shadow
Working through obstacles, trials to endure, carrying a burden, distancing oneself from your clan, needing to fortify one's inner structure

Stirring the Mystic Cauldron

When Divining, These Align with Nyd
The sun sign: Capricorn
The card: The Devil
The archetype: The authority

Qualities They Share
Finances, focus, responsibility, maturity

11. Is
English translation: ice

Frozen water was a familiar guest in the cold winters of northern European rune societies. Since ice was a normal occurrence during the long cold season, people knew to prepare for its presence. It was not an unwelcome foe, but a regular visitor who knocked on the door, and they learned to make the best of it. Although it could be potentially treacherous, for those with foresight the challenges that severe frost brought could be met with success. Hence, when Is—the rune that embraces the moon, its changing cycles, feminine energy, the intuition, and the archetype of the divine maiden—was divined, it brought a prognosis: if you want to walk with strength, be prepared to listen with your instincts and feel your way to making the right choices.

When Is appears in your rune cast, life is asking you to know how to walk the wintry ice that covers the river waters. Prepare to protect your dreams and nourish your thirst. Chances are, changes or delays are coming, but even so, you can reflect on ways to move forward and improve any situation you might be facing.

The bridge that the divine maiden crosses to become a mother before evolving to a crone is built on a foundation of wisdom through experience. In Norse mythology, the goddess Hel, daughter of Loki, rules the icy underworld of the dishonored dead. She is said to be a half-beautiful maiden with a beguiling motherly smile and half-troll-like crone with magical powers. Her lunar nature brings a warning not to play on ice without knowing how to find your way safely across it. Confidence to follow her "It will all be okay" attitude requires summoning your Viking might to trust your instincts to feel your way safely across the frozen water and not misstep to a deathly plunge by falling through thin ice. Worldly insights through soulful, intuitive reflections—energies that you can tap into as you merge with the voice of the oracle—exist within your nonlinear realm.

Keywords for Is

The Self

Strong intuition, dreams bring important messages, truths may be tested, efforts meet icy reception, the need to protect one's self

The Shadow

Emotional complexities, facing a situational or actual ice storm, being distracted from core issues, traveling uncharted territory

Is cannot be reversed. But it can be read with shadow interpretations if it falls with a downward slant.

Stirring the Mystic Cauldron

When Divining, These Align with Is

The planet: The moon
The card: The High Priestess
The archetype: The divine maiden

Qualities They Share

The feminine, esoterica, nurturing, dreams

12. Ger
English translation: harvest

Ger is significant of the turning of the seasons, a certain length of time, or a completed time when the harvest of efforts can be gathered. As an archetype of the Sage, this rune represents reaping the rewards of inner work to gain insight into the soul. Whatever seeds you have sown in the past, it's time to celebrate your earthly cornucopia and enjoy the tangible rewards for the completion of your work.

Although this rune most often indicates a positive direction, because of the dualistic nature of life, harvest season may or may not be as fruitful as you hope. Even if Skadi, the Norse goddess of winter, is known to have a warm heart, she can lose her sense of timing while having too much fun skiing in the mountains and leave the cold northern winter winds to rush early into the season. Mother Nature can hold back the frost giants for only so long before they'll freeze the life-sustaining plants and herbs in one's garden. With awareness, it's the beauty and love for the work you do that protects your efforts from unexpected woes.

Whether your goals are for material or spiritual prosperity, submerge dreams and longings into your passion and organize resources to accomplish what will bring the most benefit to you and yours. Regardless of the uncertainties of life, your internal know-how to make the best of life enables you to gather joy during your endeavors. When feeling gratitude for your blessings, your inner sage doesn't need to balance your budget to know how wealthy you are within. This rune acts like a charm for connecting with your inner shaman, sage, or muses for guidance on how to best reach for the stars to increase your celestial illumination.

Keywords for Ger

The Self
Completing a cycle, harvest time, picking the fruits of your labor, productivity, happiness, service to a worthy cause, financial clarity

The Shadow
Overthinking, worrying about outcomes, getting distracted, ignoring the natural cycles of life or your wisdom about your body

Stirring the Mystic Cauldron

When Divining, These Align with Ger
The sun sign: Virgo
The card: The Hermit
The archetype: The sage

Qualities They Share
Analyzing, finances, harvest, wisdom

13. Eoh
English translation: the yew

Eoh is the time-honored sign of the strength and endurance compared with the branches of the life-giving Yew tree, symbol of eternal life. To the ancients, the yew was sacred because it attracted the enchanted beings of the fairy kingdoms. Magical, it was thought to protect the spirits of the dead and ease the stress of passing between the worlds.

When this rune is selected, it's a message to search for a sacred site, either inwardly or externally, where you can honor your intentions and contemplate what stays dear to your heart and what no longer serves you. It's important to step up to the tasks that are awaiting your attention. By turning inward, you can meditatively look with your sixth sense to find answers to heal the wounds of the past, and to open your mind to dive into fresh spring waters of renewal.

Eoh, similar to the sun sign Scorpio and the archetypal phoenix rising from the ashes, is a reminder not to be afraid of change. You can experience the beauty of personal evolution only through traversing uncharted fields of personal growth and emotional exploration. Self-discovery comes from quenching your thirst by drinking from the sacred well, where life's mysteries can be solved through nonverbal intuitive perceptions.

If you sense that the truth of your convictions is being tested by change, calm your concerns through reflection on your inward journey. You may have to wait until the water of life clears before you can fully see and understand the opportunities that are arising on the horizon.

Keywords for Eoh

The Self
Rebirth, death, change, magical perceptions, strong emotion, reincarnation, finding hidden resources, penetrating the depths

The Shadow
The need for protection, moodiness, emotional complexity, facing trials of change or revenge

Stirring the Mystic Cauldron

When Divining, These Align with Eoh
The sun sign: Scorpio
The card: Death
The archetype: The phoenix

Qualities They Share
Rebirth, transformation, intensity, emotional

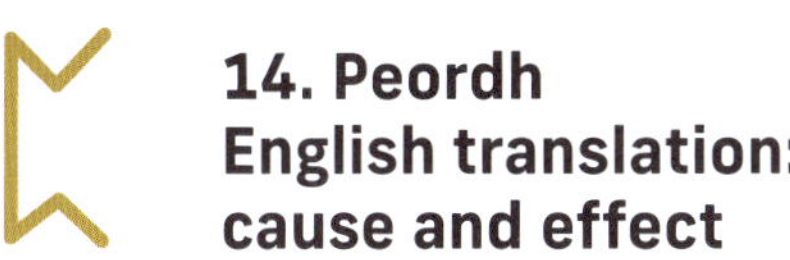

14. Peordh English translation: cause and effect

In olden days, for those seeking clarity and direction concerning their life journey, decision-making would often be delayed until the oracles had been consulted. When Peordh, the rune compared to a dice cup and the drawing of lots, appeared in a rune cast, it was a sign to call upon the voices of the three Fays of Destiny, the Norns. These wise ones, known as the Weird Sisters, who lived in a cosmic cave at the base of the World Tree, would weave threads of fate by using their unlimited knowledge of what was, what is, and what shall be, and show the way to a better understanding of the laws of nature and the mysterious passage between Midgard (Earth) and Asgard (home of the gods).

Even after the passing of many centuries, the importance of this rune embodies the wise elder archetypal forces of time and its hourglass law of cause and effect. The Saturnian overview of karmic measures culminating in Peordh points to the unalterable hand that holds tight the reins of reward and punishment. The nonjudgmental power between action and reaction brings lessons to fine-tune messages from your head and heart and to clarify bonds with kin and clan, friends and partners, and your higher self.

The more you trust the messages transmitted from your sixth sense, the greater your chances for perceiving bone-solid truths of your here-and-now reality and where you're going in the future. When you throw this rune, following the straight and narrow path of your heart's truth will set you free to go in the right direction, even if there's a caution sign ahead.

Keywords for Peordh

The Self
Self-examination, listening to inner truth, an unfolding resolution, acknowledging your own authority, following rules, karma in action

The Shadow
Restrictive boundaries, being short of time, facing a karmic lesson, financial or travel concerns, an unlucky roll of the dice

Stirring the Mystic Cauldron

When Divining, These Align with Peordh
The planet: Saturn
The card: The World
The archetype: The wise elder

Qualities They Share
Karma, values, responsibility, limits

15. Eolh
English translation: hope

The ancients believed that this sign would bring protection from worldly harm or misfortune, and they engraved it on shields of battle, amulets, and temple archways. Rune authorities speculate on the original significance of its shape—a straight line with three upward branches—and have analyzed it as the following: a hand holding three fingers heavenward in a sign of defense; the claws of birds of prey, such as a falcon or hawk, honored for their fierce might and strength; the powerful and protecting horns of the elk; and the sharp, cutting blades of eelgrass, a water plant found in England's marshes.

Eolh's three fingers are significant of reaching beyond known boundaries so that you can listen to messages from the wind, know how far you must go to find drinking water, or know what you must know to capture the messages from the stars. Just as the Aesir gods of the eldest rune societies blessed humanity with three gifts—Spirit, will, and warmth, this important symbol points to the archetype of an inspirited force within you that can utilize these treasures to bring you ever closer to the fulfillment of your purpose and peace of mind.

When Eolh is cast, it's often a sign of nurturing and protection, qualities connected with the sun sign Cancer. It can also be a signal to use your intuition to view what choices are best for you. Persistent efforts to find your right path replace life's uncertainties and lead to the confidence needed to release what no longer serves you. It's time to surrender your trust to higher powers. Invisible forces are being manipulated by the unseen hand of universal forces to enhance and protect your worldly and spiritual growth.

Keywords for Eolh

The Self
Intuition, opportunities to create success, being nurtured, protection from harm, connecting with your higher self

The Shadow
Uncertainty, concerns about safety, unwanted change, insecurity, anxieties, not listening to your intuition or instincts

Stirring the Mystic Cauldron

When Divining, These Align with Eolh
The sun sign: Cancer
The card: The Chariot
The archetype: The nurturer

Qualities They Share
Receptivity, protection, change, clairvoyance

16. Sigel
English translation: the sun

An auspicious rune, Sigel, equated with the sun, indicates success, inspiration, and regeneration. When you consider the importance of the sun to the runic communities, it's easy to understand why it is considered one of the most fortunate runes. The sun brought the welcoming light into an often-gloomy, wintry world where dangers and sorcery were common. Its brilliance chased away the dark, lessening the fear of what may be hiding in the shadows. Its healing rays nourished the body as well as the spirit of joy and laughter. Bringing relief from the cold northern winds, the sun warmed the earth so that life-nourishing seeds could sprout.

There are many celebrations of life centered on this fiery orb. People worshiped it and its mighty gods as protectors who listened to their prayers and illuminated their hopes for the continuation of the unbroken thread of life. One popular Norse sun goddess, Sol, was sister to Mani, god of the moon. Her power to heal and offer safekeeping were immortalized in stories handed down by word of mouth from early times. Another was the Celtic sun god, Belenos, who was called upon for his magical incantations and the healing power of his light.

In modern rune casting, Sigel implies that the value of positive thinking inspires hope and victory over struggles. A mirror to the archetype of the self, Sigel helps you see who you are when stripped naked to your conscious core, and puts light on your understanding of how to feel whole within yourself. It's comparable to the sun peeking out from behind a cloud, brightening moods so that darkness will diminish. It's an illuminating omen to keep an open mind to sharing your spirit's light with the world.

Keywords for Sigel

The Self
Hope, victory, light, overcoming fear, the unleashing of powerful forces, renewal, inspiration, creative insights, warmth, vibrant energy

The Shadow
Not owning your personal power, lack of confidence or clarity, needing to lighten up, take time to find some sunshine

Stirring the Mystic Cauldron

When Divining, These Align with Sigel
The planet: The sun
The card: The Sun
The archetype: The self

Qualities They Share
Vitality, creativity, children, happiness

↑ 17. Tyr English translation: victory

Tyr shares its name with the Norse god of war, who negotiated laws and treaties with fiery courage and astute wisdom. The importance of this symbol was so great that it was engraved on warrior's swords and shields as a sign of the power to conquer the enemy and fight under the protective force of the divine. Victory over the struggles of life and death came to those whose faith trusted in its heroic might.

Tyr, a sign to invoke the willingness to fight for what is right and have the strength and the mental sharpness to keep the trolls and giants at bay, brings good fortune to those who hold it close. Success comes when determination is strong enough to pursue personal victory until battles are won, and goals—be they intellectual, emotional, or physical—can be reached. Chanting the sound of Tyr with courage and independent-mindedness (Aries qualities) empowers one to readily conquer struggles, even during life's fierce storms.

Its influence awakens the dawn of understanding and lights the path to a fulfilling destiny. Comparable to The Emperor, leadership and having the motivation to win is key to taking the throne of command and wielding the sword of success. Both the archetypes of the fiery warrior and the prominent leader share a connection with Tyr, depending on what powers are being called to duty. Not only does this rune share its name with the god who was one of the most dominant in the ancient northern realms, but it also has the honor of ruling over the third aett, the last group of runes in the Elder Futhark. Its mark, the upward-pointing arrow, is a reminder to look up and invite the infinite into your life.

Keywords for Tyr

The Self
Victory over conflicts, power, strength of mind, working out negotiations, fair-mindedness, finding harmony, protection of honor

The Shadow
Struggles with leadership or power issues, needing to take a stand or reevaluate what's right, conflicts with dragons, disagreements

Stirring the Mystic Cauldron

When Divining, These Align with Tyr
The sun sign: Aries
The card: The Emperor
The archetype: The leader

Qualities They Share
Strong will, ambition, courage, independence

18. Beorc English translation: a budding birch

Beorc embodies the springtime of love, blessed with mirth and hopefulness for what tomorrow will bring. It's the inner stirrings of the archetypal Eros, channeling fervent emotions into alluring pools of romantic enchantment, creativity, and transformation. A sign of birth, it's comparable to a dormant seed being fertilized with Mother Nature's power to seduce and sprout anew. It embodies the delights of finding love, passion's play, and courting rituals.

Aligned with the noble qualities of Freyja, Norse goddess of love, nurturing, beauty, fertility, sensuality, and tenderheartedness, Beorc shines the welcoming light of positive energy. When it appears in your rune cast, it's a good time to access emotional needs and to think about what you want and the temptations of its potential reality. The need to be self-accepting, patient, and calm is a worthy step to consider when you are making efforts to help your passion soar into a tangible form.

Auspicious, Beorc indicates a favorable direction. There's no better time than now to stir the bubbling cauldron of life-affirming intentions to win the war against frustrations and woes. Your positive efforts are comparable to invocations to Odin to open the 540 doors to Valhalla, the greatest of his buildings, fit to house heroes and kings, and allow dreams of happiness to enter.

Keywords for Beorc

The Self
Abundance; creative pursuits; fertility of mind, body, or spirit; living one's passion; potential for love, marriage, and pregnancy

The Shadow
Worries about outcomes, tension in relations, emotional stress or insecurities, unproductivity, stifled creativity

Stirring the Mystic Cauldron

When Divining, These Align with Beorc
The planet: Venus
The card: The Empress
The archetype: Eros

Qualities They Share
Love, beauty, pleasure, happiness

ᛗ

19. Eh English translation: a horse or two horses

To the ancients, horses were equal to celestial beings. In myths and legends, they were thought to have healing and transcendental power and could pull the chariots of the gods. Odin's mythic, muscular, eight-legged gray steed, Sleipnir, was known to ride with the wind in this world and in the realm of death. In practical reality, his ownership brought prestige and communicated a message of otherworldly prosperity.

Eh, considered by some to be a sign of a divine union and soulmates, represents dual forces, such as the Gemini twins, mortality and immortality, the waking mind and the dreaming mind, or two horses pulling in opposing directions. Its archetypal message signifies balancing different energies such as the sweet and the sour, acceptance and rejection, and the head and the heart, in order to create a sense of harmony and strengthen communications. When it appears in your cast, it's a sign that you may need to sort out right from wrong and what direction is best, and to say yes or no to continue trekking along your current path.

Trained or untamed, horses are symbols of power, speed, mobility, exploration, and travel. When harnessed, they have the galloping stamina to transport heavy loads over long distances. The faster the horse, the higher the rider's status; the stronger the horse, the more powerful the rider in battle. It's comparable to the symbol of your inner steed supporting your responsibilities, and you may be forced to widen your perspective on your commitments and balance expectations with worldly possibilities. It's time to increase your stride and ride the soaring winds of awareness to find your path to a perfect destiny.

Keywords for Eh

The Self
Inspiration to advance, strong communications, marriage or union, harmony, taking the right path, potentials activated

The Shadow
Lack of harmony, loosening ties or partnerships, not making the right choice, miscommunications, frustrated travel plans

Stirring the Mystic Cauldron

When Divining, These Align with Eh
The sun sign: Gemini
The card: The Lovers
The archetype: The messenger

Qualities They Share
Unity, messages, choices, duality

20. Mann English translation: man

In Norse mythology, in the beginning times there existed only the Aesir gods. As their creativity stirred, these gods envisioned the possibilities of mankind. Using the forms of the alder and ash trees, they designed and gave birth to man and woman. Mann is the rune signifying the evolving race of humankind and the power of the mind to reflect the wisdom of the gods. When you hold it in your hand and call its name to the wind, trust that the spirits will answer, if you are willing to listen. Its subtle magic is comparable to the sublime attributes of the mind: the ability to think, reason, and remember, and the cognizance of becoming more today than you were yesterday. For those living in olden times, its mundane power was equal to having the wisdom to gather life-giving moss, bark, fruit, and nuts, and to know how to fish and hunt to win the struggles of survival.

Similar to the archetype of the reformer, it signifies taking time for contemplation and becoming more aware of how to best voice your truth and stand strong against crashing waves of change. The hidden gems of your intuitive insights are your mightiest weapons against unexpected affairs that may be coming your way.

Mann is comparable to empowering your confidence to fulfill your commitments and evolving dreams of who you are becoming. Rethinking responsibilities and wielding the sword of your truth unleashes vital potentials for knowing how best your mind and body can thrive.

Keywords for Mann

The Self
Mental inspiration, finding fresh insights, plans are improved, the dawning of a brighter reality, serendipity, making new friends

The Shadow
Faulty logic, lack of perception, disagreements, impulsive actions, plans may be disrupted

Stirring the Mystic Cauldron

When Divining, These Align with Mann
The sun sign: Aquarius
The card: The Star
The archetype: The reformer

Qualities They Share
Humanitarian, upbeat, empathy, freedom

21. Lagu
English translation: water

Lagu signals the importance of being in touch with your gut instincts and trusting the flowing, fluctuating currents in the River of Life. To the ancients, its mark was a connection with the magical undines or water sprites, who had ghostlike appearances and lived hidden within nature's lake and river environments. Extremely beautiful, they were irresistible and could seduce humans to swim in waves of mystery to unknown shores, from where they might never return. If a Viking seeress or sybil could communicate with the life-sustaining power of water, she could create spells, charms, and talismans and exercise her right to see the future, ease difficulties, and influence the will of humankind.

In current times, this rune is often interpreted as the wellspring of inspiration, a water force that erodes the sharp edges from complexities deep within the subconscious. Practically, it is viewed in connection with thirst-relieving gifts of the water, but symbolically it's linked with feelings, romantic fantasies, the intuitive qualities of the archetypal mystic who can sense what lies under the surface of emotions. True to its Neptunian nature, it benefits those using or developing their intuition and those who are willing to dive into the realms of ritual and sacred mysteries.

Whatever your mystical mode, or even your distance from it, Lagu can toss you a life raft that enables an instinctual flow toward renewal and a fresh understanding of truth. It signals listening to the undercurrent in the messages that your senses feel in the moment, and being alert to seeing with your third eye. Finding the pathway to the fulfillment of your dreams depends upon it.

Keywords for Lagu

The Self
Surfing the ebb and flow of emotions, receptivity to evolutionary thinking, trusting your intuition, subtle vibrations, austerities

The Shadow
Riding powerful waves of emotions, confusion, not seeing a situation clearly, needing to be more logical

Stirring the Mystic Cauldron

When Divining, These Align with Lagu
The planet: Neptune
The card: The Hanged Man
The archetype: The mystic

Qualities They Share
Dreams, illusion, intuition, nonconformity

22. Ing English translation: fertility

Before Christianity become dominant, Ing was the name of the fertility god who was worshiped as the divine spark and inspiration for the germinating forces of life and renewal. The rune bearing this enchanted name is connected with the thawing of ice, the blossoms of new growth, and rebirth. A catalyst for change, it's also compared to the male scrotum, generator of life-giving seeds planted with the heated fires of desire and passion. Used for rites of passage, love spells, and sex magic, the sign of Ing is loaded with magical potency.

A subtle yet vibrant force, like fuel for the soul, it can involve spiritual regeneration and dormant or mysterious powers. When selected, Ing is a signal to finish uncompleted tasks and current projects so that your energy can give birth to new possibilities and travel to unexplored psychic spaces. Freeing your tethers to emotional complexities enables you to say a happy goodbye to yesterday, transition into the new, and become more available to take advantage of change.

Ing's potency may be invisible, but it's bonded with the miraculous that converts gross matter into spirited opportunities to turn decay and stagnation into rebirth, repose, and resurrection. Listening with your heart to its message can soften your receptivity to its purpose in your rune cast and illuminate its underlying meaning.

Keywords for Ing

The Self
Rebirth, transition into the new, spiritual or magical upliftment, facing the unknown, entering unfamiliar space, finding an amulet or magical tool

The Shadow
Feeling judged unfairly, unwanted changes, facing dark forces, generational arguments, betrayal or guilt, complex sexual issues

Stirring the Mystic Cauldron

When Divining, These Align with Ing
The planet: Pluto
The card: Judgement
The archetype: Rebirth

Qualities They Share
Transformation, disruption, the subconscious, mystery

23. Daeg English translation: daylight

In olden days, Daeg was a sign to protect oneself against evil spirits, trolls, and other creatures looming in the dark. Its otherworldly potency could conjure a magical wrap of warmth and confidence with a shielding energy that opened possibilities for laughter and life-sustaining endurance. It was a strong defense against the frost giants, and its influence conjured an alchemical sphere of positive forces comparable to the coming of the light of day after a long night.

Daeg is linked with the Norse god Baldr, son of the god Odin and the high-ranking goddess wife Frigg. He was known for his innocence, purity, peace, and joy, and his supernatural wisdom shined a protective glow on the slippery, stepping-stoned journey to the four corners of the nine worlds, where bewitching incantations echo amid the sounds of the god's laughter.

Just like Baldr utilized light to chase away enemies, Daeg calls on you to use your inner light to chase away darkness and destroy anxieties that cast dark shadows over your joy. It's a reminder to let go of worries and find your center, where you can stand strong against adverse forces. With this rune comes the message to let your spirit soar free and dance with the wind. Focus on friends and activities that encourage your sense of empowerment. If you aren't sure if you've made the right choices or if you feel you may need to change past decisions, the dawning of fresh insights will illuminate the direction you need to go. The message this stone carries is to celebrate the many gifts you are given, for you are blessed more than you realize.

Keywords for Daeg

The Self
Freeing your mind from worries, enthusiasm, living in harmony, being in the now, nonconformity, individuality, alchemy

The Shadow
Loss of freedom, going against authority, upset with other's demands, eccentricity, unexpected detour

Stirring the Mystic Cauldron

When Divining, These Align with Daeg
The planet: Uranus
The card: The Fool
The archetype: The child

Qualities They Share
The unexpected, freedom, innovation, unrest

24. Ethel English translation: property

In early times, Ethel was associated with the land and protected spaces where migrating tribes could settle, garden, hunt, and create a more stable homelife. It inspired a sense of security, protection from otherworldly spirits, and safety for one's family and clan. Ideas concerning one's origin, shucked like wheat from the chaff, put life in order and helped one's understanding of the ways of the gods, the rules of nature, and the might of tyrants' weapons.

For modern rune casters, it's likely to inspire a message about security in the heart and home, the value of intellectual and physical property, and the getting or releasing of desires and possessions. Its power nurtures the flow of experiences that helps you develop skills, advance forward, and stir the cauldron of endless possibilities. A mirror to the enchantments of the archetypal young maiden, Ethel also involves investigating the mysteries of one's soulful self and seeking insight into one's ancestral inheritance.

Closing the door to the body of knowledge contained in the Elder Futhark, this last rune shines on truths deeply rooted within the cavernous, subconscious mind. Holding its symbol close to your heart can make it easier to view the psychic landscape where you carry ideas and beliefs conditioned by earlier generations and family values. It's a reminder not to fight the lessons encountered early in one's life, but to take advantage of them in order to build a strong core of love and self-acceptance in this moment, even if you're dreaming about where you might go in the future.

Keywords for Ethel

The Self
Increasing stability, finding an emotional comfort zone, buying property, building a home, developing intuitive potentials, connecting with ancestral wisdom

The Shadow
Being tethered by responsibilities, feeling unsettled, family issues, looking for property, the need for emotional centering or becoming intuitively grounded

Stirring the Mystic Cauldron

When Divining, These Align with Ethel
The planet: The waxing moon
The card: The High Priestess
The archetype: The maiden

Qualities They Share
Property, depth, memories, clairvoyance

PART FOUR

DIVINATION'S DOORWAY

CHAPTER 9

WALKING THROUGH MYSTICAL DOORWAYS

Previously, we explored important building blocks for discussing the most-important components of the zodiac, Major Arcana cards, and runestones. Compared with traditional astrological meanings, archetypes and key qualities are presented as common denominators to help you recognize the overlapping threads of interpretative possibilities among the three systems.

Once you become familiar with the stars, cards, and stones and can recognize shared universal themes that weave unity among these three mystical arts, you can begin to develop your divination skills by using these three oracles. Or, perhaps you solely want to learn to use these mediums as tools for self-discovery. Whatever way you decide to use your oracles, if you keep the attitude of a fearless deep-sea diver, working with them becomes easier every time you practice. Experience will be one of your most important teachers. It will help you learn to listen with your inner ear and meaningfully connect with each sun sign, card, and runestone. With a commitment to let your mind freely submerge into a "reading space," you'll find answers to questions that are beyond the grasp of your logic.

Some people need to take baby steps into the unpredictable world of giving readings. Others may quickly jump into unknown divinatory channels with a burst of confident, star-bright buoyancy. Whatever feels right for you is where to begin. Don't force yourself to work any form of divination until you feel ready. Your creativity, courage, and good instincts mixed with the sweat of beginning to practice divination will determine the speed in which you feel comfortable offering interpretations. Mixed with the power of your desire to interpret messages in the stars, cards, and runes, your ability to hear their meaningful silence will come as you walk through the time tunnel called Play and Practice.

Let your instincts be your guide for when and where you divine, and if you should or shouldn't read for someone. If you feel that you don't want to do a reading, just say, "No!" Trust what you feel as your spontaneous truth, even if your feelings go against someone else's request. To succeed in doing this work, you'll need to listen to your instincts and, importantly, follow them.

Usually, the more readings you do, the more your understanding of symbols grows and your intuitive skills evolve. Developing your intuition is equal to trying to strengthen any muscle, which will get noticeably stronger as you continue to exercise it. Without looking into a crystal ball, I can tell you with certainty that it's your faith in yourself and your confidence that will give you the green light for traveling the etheric freeway of divination.

Don't overcomplicate or justify your interpretations. Many of your insights can weave heartfelt discussions and a positive exchange between you and your client. Be prepared to respond nonjudgmentally to life's dramas as you become a firsthand witness to testimonies of life at its finest and its worst. You may hear challenging questions involving domestic or child abuse, lovers splitting apart, betrayal, adultery, dysfunctionality, incurable disease, and impending loss.

> Discovering how to divine comes from quenching your thirst by drinking from the overflowing cup of the sacred.

GETTING READY TO DIVINE

As you continue following along with these lessons, it's essential that you have your cards and stones within reach. If you want to know how to do the card and stone layouts, it's helpful for you to practice doing them as you view their demonstration.

If you're planning to do readings for others, you're going to need to practice self-care and learn to take extra good care of yourself as well as your oracles. One common method is psychic cleansing, by smudging with fragrant sage or sweetgrass. Similar to lighting incense in a safe holder, you light a small piece of your herb and let its smoke purify the air. Blow the smoke around your working space, your oracles, and yourself. While doing so, you might imagine a healing light surrounding you, and mentally set positive intentions for your and your client's well-being. In my practice, I inwardly affirm that I'm becoming a clear channel for receiving messages that will benefit my client. I also silently ask my muses to guard my working circle from uninvited interruptions.

Doing a centering meditation or chanting, praying, or singing can also add to your sense of harmony and help you feel safe, comfortable, and grounded when reading for another. Sitting with your spine straight and your feet flat on the floor is a good reminder to keep your communications rooted to the earth.

If you're overly empathic and supersensitive to another person's energy, you can find resources to study psychic self-defense techniques, so that when you read the Devil card, or the rune Nyd, you can work through their potentially challenging messages in a calm and centered manner. When discussing sensitive issues, it's possible that your client will start crying. Don't look alarmed. Offer support and have your emotional boundaries in place so that you don't start crying as well. When you're looking through your third eye, a good attitude is your best ally to keep communications flowing clearly and hopefully.

Being a voice for oracles requires inner vision as well as common sense. Doing readings will automatically open your mind and senses for reading "vibes" or energy. When a client first sits with you, what are your impressions of this person? Do you sense anything that might influence your reading? Do you inwardly hear any unspoken messages? Don't ignore your gut instincts when you first meet someone. They may hold important messages and offer clues for how to best read the person sitting in front of you.

Following are some phrases that can be used to set positive intentions before you begin working with your oracles.

Affirmations for Encouragement

Affirm: I empower myself to give meaningful readings.
Acknowledge: I can do this!
Positive visualization: I am opening my third eye and becoming more intuitive.
Or: I see myself successfully reading the stars, the cards, and the stones.

Preparing Your Worktable

Find a quiet space. Consider turning your intended reading area into a sacred area where people will enjoy lingering. Unless you're sitting on the ground, you'll need a table, an attractive tablecloth, and a few chairs. The following items are optional: candles, flowers, crystals, and pictures or statues of whoever inspires you. You can put anything that makes you feel good in your reading room. If you have aromatherapy sprays for creating harmony, psychic alignment, protection, or channeling the gods, have them within reach. Your cards and stones should be near you in their protective cloth, bag, or box. If any are wrapped in a sizable cloth, consider using it to lay out your cards or stones (or both) when giving your readings.

For a moment, look from within your third eye to connect with the vibrations of your space. How does your decorated table with your cards and stones feel? Is it tempting or not? Is there anything you can add to make it feel more inviting?

Selecting Cards and Stones

When you're ready to start your reading, take your cards or stones out of their pouch, cloth, or box. Silently, take a few deep, relaxing breaths. It can help your focus to do a short meditation to clear your mind of your personal concerns and ask your guides, angels, or muses to bless your work with the clarity and foresight to help guide your client.

If you're at the early stages of offering to do readings for others, you'll most likely want your client to ask their question out loud. When you're on your way to being a pro, it's fascinating to have your client silently think their question and then let the oracle provide its answer. It's your choice whether to let a person shuffle your cards or toss your runes, or whether you perform these necessary rituals for your client.

When you interpret reversed cards and stones in your readings, one suggestion is to limit how many are given reversed interpretations. If more than one-third of your cards or stones appear reversed, use your common sense when interpreting them so that your reading doesn't make your clients feel like their world is turned upside down. It's disappointing when someone goes to a reader hoping to increase clarity, and then they walk away from their session with a foreboding sense of doom. Whenever possible, find helpful insights for your client's concerns and emphasize options for a hopeful tomorrow.

The truth is that we all sometimes have conflicts, but when doing a reading try not to focus on the anxiety-producing aspects of life (unless it benefits your reading). When interpreting a rune or a card that indicates difficulty, look at nearby supporting runes or cards to see how they may benefit offering constructive or healing insights for your querent.

Cutting Your Cards

There are different methods for cutting cards. Try different approaches and have fun experimenting with various possibilities to get a sense of what methods work best for you. Even after you have given many readings and have developed your personal style, you can still discover new ways to cut your deck.

While my cards are being shuffled, I ask my client to silently think about their situation and concerns. After the cards have been shuffled, I usually have my client cut them into three stacks in a horizontal row on the table. Then, I take the cards from the middle stack, turn over the top card, and begin my reading. The number of cards I take from this stack will depend on the spread I'm using.

Also, you can have your client shuffle the cards and cut them in four (or six or nine) stacks. And then you can turn over the top card in each stack and offer your interpretations.

When I'm using only the Major Arcana cards in my reading, I usually won't have people cut my cards. After my shuffle, I'll fan all twenty-two downward-facing cards in a horizontal row and ask my client to use their intuition to select a card for each card position in the spread. For example, I'll say, "Use your intuition and select a card that feels best for insight into your present situation." Or, "The next card you select will highlight your feelings concerning your current issues."

Casting the Runes

Before casting the runes, I meditatively ask my inner self to sense my client's energy. After shaking my pouch and tossing the stones, I will create the rune cast in a systematic order that feels most appropriate in the moment.

If I'm reading for friends, I'm less formal in my approach. Because I often know their concerns, to get our conversation flowing I'll reach into my rune bag and instinctively pull out several stones and lay each one face up on the table in a horizontal row. If I'm working with someone I don't know, I'll set all my runes face down on my table. I'll have this person ask their question either out loud or silently. I'll ask them to randomly select several or more runes to provide the insight on how best to answer their question. After the downward-facing stones are selected, I'll turn them face upward, place them in a circle or other pattern, and let our reading begin.

If I have more time, I'll use a ritualistic approach. I'll have all of my stones facing downward on the center of the table. I'll ask my client to silently think about their concerns and, while doing so, to use their left hand to move the stones in a clockwise circle three times. If a stone accidentally turns itself upright during this shuffle, I let it stay that way. The meaning of the stone or stones that do this will be interpreted during the reading.

After the client is finished moving the stones in a circle, he or she is asked to intuitively select stones and place them face up on the table. Often a person will ask where to place them. If I want the stones aligned in a specific design, I will put them in place or explain where each belongs.

When doing readings, some readers let their clients spontaneously place their selected runes in any way they choose, and then they evaluate the symbolic pattern of the rune's placement. The unique design of the layout becomes an additional clue to interpret during the reading. Another approach is to simply take your rune pouch, give it a few magical shakes, and toss all the runes on the table. Let them sit where they fall, and read each stone that lies upright.

As you look at each faceup rune, it will be pointing up or down to some degree. You must determine if its direction is up, sideways, slightly downward, or completely reversed. If the stone is pointing mostly upward, consider it upright. If it is only slightly upward, your interpretation should be slanted to include reversed possibilities equal to the degree of its downward tilt. If the rune faces downward, it should be viewed as a reversed rune. When viewing the positions of the rune symbols, your decisions about the degree of their slant and how to best interpret them are your subjective observation.

READING THE CARDS AND STONES

You can offer short readings—maybe fifteen minutes or less, or you can spend much more time and dive into them with lengthy depth. The amount of time it takes for you to give a reading is up to you and your client. Giving a reading is like telling a story with a beginning, a middle, and an end. Either you can give a reading as a monologue, or you can interact with your client and have a dialogue that includes reflections and responses to your interpretations. How you structure your readings depends on what you deem important, and your time, energy, and inclinations.

> Don't overthink how to do divination. Having confidence is the first thing you need. You can't do readings without it.

The readings that accompany the following discussions are not hypothetical illustrations, but questions that people have asked me during readings. I'm presenting these illustrations to help you have a sense of what issues might underlie a person's request for a reading. People's names have been altered to honor the reader's code of client confidentiality.

All the spreads and rune casts illustrated in the following pages can be equally created using either the cards or stones. For example, if you want to work with your runes instead of the cards when you are reading instructions for a specific card spread, toss your stones and use them in place of your cards while you follow with the card spread instructions and discussion.

Readings with One-Card and One-Stone Sun Signs

For people who judge the one-card spread or one-stone rune cast as being too simple, they're missing the magic of how much can be learned about one's client in a single image. The one-card spread or single-stone rune cast is most often used for answering a short question. It can also be used to break the ice with a client before giving a longer reading.

Your answer during a short reading should be brief because you need to interpret only one card or stone. If your discussion becomes too long, most likely you'll be drawing more cards and stones to answer more questions. Narrow your focus to the one question and trust that you can find a meaningful brief answer to share.

You can start a one-card or one-stone reading by asking your client whether he or she has a question. It's your choice to have the person ask their question out loud or silently in his or her mind. The practice is simple. Either you or your person shuffles and cuts the cards or throws your stones. After a card or a stone is selected and viewed, it's time to interpret its message. Listen to the ideas and feelings that come into your mind concerning the image you are viewing.

If, when doing real-life readings, a person's question does not relate to the designated card or stone that has been selected, it may be necessary to start over and select a different card or stone. And yes, this may feel a bit awkward, but remember to enjoy the moment and forge ahead. Your role as the voice for your oracle is to offer benefit, not to get caught up in thoughts of doing psychic gymnastics. (This insight comes from the multitude of times I've had to awkwardly smile and answer the question "Are you a *real* psychic?")

The card and stone interpretations in each of the following twelve sun sign readings use one common keyword. Each keyword can be found in the section titled "Qualities They Share" in the star, card, and stone discussions within the Mystical Library. The keywords used in the following examples are written in italics to show you how divinatory arts share thematic concepts.

While reading the short questions and answers, if you're willing, take a few moments and practice giving your own replies to each of the twelve questions. This practice can help you develop your understanding of how to discuss interpretations.

Star, rune, and card representations of the Sun.

Sun Sign Readings

Aries, the Ram

Astrological quality: *Strong will*
Question asked: Will I have success in my career?
Tarot card: The Emperor
Reader's reply: The fiery Emperor indicates connecting with your personal power and focusing your ambitions and *strong will* toward creating success.
Runestone: Tyr
Reader's reply: It's a good time to work on your career goals. Tyr indicates directing your *strong will* with an active power equal to Thor's hammer in order to move forward in your career and achieve greater success.

Taurus, the Bull

Astrological quality: *Determination*
Question asked: Will I be able to become a professional singer?
Tarot card: High Priest
Reader's reply: It's important to hold on to your *determination* and follow your dreams to reach your goal. Channel your soul spirit into your music, and, like the High Priest, you'll become inspirational.
Runestone: Ur
Reader's reply: Ur is connecting with your strength and *determination* to becoming a shining star. Put your passion into your music and sing your way to performing in front of an audience.

Gemini, the Twins

Astrological quality: *Duality*
Question asked: Is my girlfriend faithful to me?
Tarot card: The Lover
Reader's reply: In this world of *duality,* people often ask, Is my lover faithful? For your peace of mind, let go of the yin and yang of your worries and enjoy being with your partner.
Runestone: Eh
Reader's reply: Sometimes when two souls dance as one, they can feel faith and fear, like sailing in Viking ships over up-and-down waves of *duality*. Listen with your instincts fully engaged to hear your heart's inner knowing of your truth and romantic direction.

Cancer, the Crab

Astrological quality: *Receptivity*
Question asked: I'm still stressed about my past relationship. I'm worried that I won't find love in the future. Will I?
Tarot card: The Chariot
Reader's reply: The Chariot's wheels are moving forward on life's path, and so are you. Don't worry about the past and the future. It's your *receptivity* to present opportunities that will help you find love again.
Runestone: Eohl
Reader's reply: When you are openhearted and have *receptivity* to connecting with others, you increase your chances for finding love. Instead of being stressed, it's time to meditate on Freyja and the light of love that shines within you.

Leo, the Lion

Astrological quality: *Vitality*
Question asked: Can you teach me to astral travel?
Tarot card: Strength
Reader's reply: You need to understand your subtle, vibrational body before you experiment with astral traveling. Meditate to strengthen your courage and spiritual *vitality* if you hope to succeed.
Runestone: Cen
Reader's reply: A courageous *vitality* is needed to astral travel. You need to know more about what it involves to determine if its nonlinear reality is within your comfort zone.

Virgo, the Virgin

Astrological quality: *Analyzing*
Question asked: I hate my stepfather. It's hopeless to talk to him about anything without getting into an argument. What should I do?
Tarot card: The Hermit
Reader's reply: Remind yourself that it is possible to talk to him if you want. When arguing, observe your feelings and endeavor to step back from reacting. Envision yourself as the sage successfully *analyzing* how to communicate with him with emotional control.
Runestone: Ger
Reader's reply: Call on Odin or a few friends whom you trust to help with *analyzing* different ways you might respond to your stepfather. Remind yourself that it is possible to learn to avoid negative confrontations if you are watchful and protect your emotions from reacting.

Libra, the Scales

Astrological quality: *Balance*
Question asked: My brother and I haven't spoken with one another for the past decade. What can you tell me about our chances for reconnecting?
Tarot card: Justice
Reader's reply: In order to reconnect with him in the present, play the role of a diplomat. Think about your brotherly love for him and *balance* positive and negative feelings to have more willingness to reach out to him.
Runestone: Gyfu
Reader's reply: Sometimes people find themselves walking a tightrope between love and hate. Strive to *balance* negative feelings with positive memories to create opportunities for healing your communications with him.

Scorpio, the Scorpion

Astrological quality: *Secretive*
Question asked: I have never met my birth father. I'm trying to find him now that I've located my birth records. Can you tell me if I'll ever meet him?
Tarot card: Death
Reader's reply: The Death card represents change, rebirth, and the potential for renewal. Hold on to your hope. Do everything you can to find him, but if he's *secretive*, he may be hiding from his past, and not be easy to find.
Runestone: Eoh
Reader's reply: Even if his information is buried in a *secretive* past, ask your intuition or angels to guide you to where he might be.

Sagittarius, the Archer

Astrological quality: *Expansion*
Question asked: Will I ever get back together with my ex-boyfriend? I still love him and can't stop thinking about our life together.
Tarot card: Temperance
Reader's reply: Temperance indicates blending positive and negative emotions and the *expansion* of understanding. If your heart wants to reconnect with your ex, seek practical ways to message him. But could it be a better use of your time to reach out and make new male friends?
Runestone: Rad
Reader's reply: Because this stone's energy is linked with *expansion*, traveling, and moving through obstacles, it points to your positive potential to improve your current life direction and find new possibilities—with or without him.

Capricorn, the Goat

Astrological quality: *Focus*
Question asked: My mother has been sick with cancer for two years. Will she ever recover?
Tarot card: The Devil
Reader's reply: It's understandable to have stress and concerns over her negative outcomes. It's mentally healthful for both of you to *focus* on her current aliveness and let your heart dwell on hopes for her recovery.
Runestone: Nyd
Reader's reply: It's understandable to worry about your mom's future. The more you stress, the less mental energy you have to *focus* on taking care both of her and yourself. Imagine a healing light encircling your mom, and take extra time to share your love with her.

Aquarius, the Water Bearer

Astrological quality: *Upbeat*
Question asked: I'm hoping to go to law school. Will I be able to become a lawyer?
Tarot card: The Star
Reader's reply: Are you willing to do the work needed? Your card, The Star, indicates the importance of *upbeat* energy. Having more optimism might help you feel more confident when you're reaching for your goal.
Runestone: Mann
Reader's reply: Imagine that an *upbeat*, inner warrior is your personal guide. He'll help you fight your pessimism and encourage you to get more in touch with your confidence to pass the required exams and become a lawyer.

Pisces, the Fish

Astrological quality: *Imagination*
Question asked: Will my business be successful?
Tarot card: The Moon
Reader's reply: Like The Moon, life has waxing and waning cycles. You need to be flexible to the ups and downs that may occur in your business. Use your *imagination* to envision yourself being successful while thriving and enjoying the high and low, pro and con, waves of business life.
Runestone: Hoegl
Reader's reply: This is the rune of the power of hail to melt into water and nourish the earth. It's also a sign to connect with magical forces and use your *imagination* to win over obstacles and become a winner in your career.

AFTER THE SPIRAL DANCE: CONVERSATIONS WITH YOUR CARDS AND STONES

The Three-Card Past, Present, Future Spread

The three-card spread is useful in answering general life questions. It offers an opportunity to look deeply yet quickly into your client's situation. This popular card spread (or rune cast) consists of three cards placed in a horizontal row after the cards have been shuffled and cut. Traditionally these cards represent the past, present, and future, or mind (thinking), emotions (feeling), and inner spirit (doing), but their positions can be assigned other meanings. For example, the first card can represent the foundation of a person's situation, the second card indicates the passive or active desire in relation to the situation, and the third card indicates the client's expectation or intended outcome. There's always the opportunity to work magic when describing the card's positions in a short spread!

Card Positions

Card 1: The first card represents the past or foundation of the situation in question. What is the beginning awareness of the concern? Who does it involve? What does the selected card suggest as the activating force behind the question? What is this card's astrological significance? How does it help you understand the person sitting in front of you?

For example, if my client selects the Fool card, I will look at her question through my lens of what I understand The Fool to represent emotionally, mentally, and spiritually. I will also consider the influence of the planet Uranus, and the archetype, the child.

Card 2: The second card sits to the right of the first card. It represents the present and offers insight into current concerns. How does this card dialogue with the first card, the card indicating your or your client's past concerns? What insights does this card offer that benefit the client's concerns? What does its astrological correspondence add to your interpretation?

Card 3: The third card sits to the right of the second card. It indicates the future direction or potential. Does it give any indication of where your client's situation is potentially going in response to their question? How does this third card influence your discussion of the previous two cards?

Your selected cards can be discussed in relation to one another, their connections with the zodiac, archetypes, and whatever else you want to include in your analysis. Many people start by reading the first card, which sits in the position titled The Past. The second card can be discussed as a reflection of the concerns in The Present. The potentials for The Future can be discussed when interpreting the symbols on the third card.

There are no rules that say you must read cards in only one sequence—your readings depend on what you see in the moment. Sometimes it's necessary to discuss whatever card jumps into view and says, "Read me first!" Readings are optimal when you follow your sense of what works best in the current moment. Allow your discussions to align with your client's needs. Watch how the cards dialogue with one another in response to your client's question. Sometimes one card will speak to you more loudly than the others and take up most of the time you have with your client.

The Cardinal Spread

This four-card spread is created by using four randomly selected cards in response to a question asked out loud or silently. Each of the four card positions is discussed as if you are placing the cards on the zodiac wheel on the four cardinal points, the cusp of the first, fourth, seventh, and tenth houses. These points sit on the vertical and horizontal axes of the horoscope: ASC, the ascendant (east, sunrise); DSC, the descendant (west, sunset); MC, the midheaven (south, noon); and IC, the nadir (north, midnight). Because these angles are of paramount importance in chart interpretation, discussing the significance of the cards highlights cardinal concerns, such as initiating ideas, important changes, and new seasons or opportunities for growth. Generally, cards placed in these four positions will help you understand what a person's energy is doing and where it appears to be going in regard to their spirit, emotions, mind, and body questions.

To begin, after you have shuffled your facedown cards and cut them, it's time to select four cards and set them on your table. Going in a counterclockwise circle, place each one on one of the four cardinal points in your envisioned zodiacal circle.

Card Positions

Card 1: This first card mirrors your sense of who your client appears to be and how you can best interpret his or her energy. Your first-card position represents the following:

First-house significance: The ascendant, how you or the client views one's inner self in relation to the question being considered, behaviors, and how others might see you or the client

Natural ruler of first house: Aries (initiating), Mars, (actions), and the fire element (creative and enterprising nature)

Card 2: Interpret the second card in response to your client's question while considering the following:

Fourth-house significance: Your client's home, inner foundation, emotions, the mother, and hopes for the second half of life

Natural ruler of fourth house: Cancer (the home), moon (the intuition), and the water element (emotions)

Card 3: The third card sits in the position of the cusp of the seventh house on the zodiac wheel. It can be interpreted in response to concerns involving the following:

Seventh-house significance: Attributes of the descendant, partnerships, lovers, marriage and deep commitments

Natural ruler of seventh house: Libra (balance), Venus (feelings), and the air element (ideas)

Card 4: Designated as the cusp of the tenth house, the fourth card should be placed at the midheaven or top of your envisioned circle. You will want to interpret the fourth selected card in response to your client's question while considering the following:

Tenth-house significance: Career success, ambitions, aspirations, and fulfillment

Natural ruler of tenth house: Capricorn (ambitions), Saturn (organization), and the earth element (finances and tangible possibilities)

CHANNELING ODIN'S LIGHT

Freyja's Trine

Three was a number of great importance in Norse mythology. The world tree Yggdrasil had three roots; there were three Norms or fates, three original beings, three monstrous children of Odin's blood brother, Loki, and three aettir in the runic alphabet; and there are many more otherworldly associations in Norse mythology. Its importance is magical.

Before you select and lay your stones to practice this rune cast, you can take three deep breaths and set the intention that you are aligning yourself with your intuition (or Odin's light). Perhaps you can light three candles and put them on your reading table to bring a sense of sacredness into your space.

Because of the magic in the number three, Freyja's trine is sure to give you an insightful rune reading. It can be used on its own to deliver a powerful message, or in addition to a previously created rune cast, such as putting Freyja's trine inside a natal-chart astrology reading. Also, it's a wonderful addition to add the magic of three stones to your Tarot card reading and do a combination

Tarot and runestone reading (think about doing combination readings only after you're comfortable reading each oracle on its own).

To begin Freyja's trine, think of your question or have your client consider his or her question while you take a moment to call upon the god, the goddess, or your muses to bring clarity to your message. If your runes are on the table, either you or your client (your choice) should take your left hand and move them in a clockwise direction several times before intuitively selecting three random runestones. The selected stones will be placed in locations that mark the three points of your envisioned runic triangle. Once the stones are positioned, it's time to begin your reading. Or, if you have your runes in a pouch, you can shake your pouch to mix the stones, then toss them onto the table. Ask your client to use his or her intuition to pick the three stones.

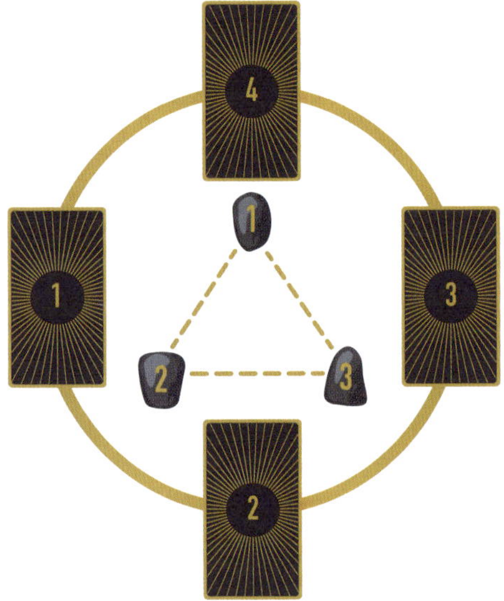

Stone Positions

Rune 1: The first stone represents you or your client in relation to Freyja's message and the "Action" (cardinal energy) needing to be taken in connection with the question being asked. It should be placed near the center of your reading table.

Rune 2: This stone is placed a couple of inches beneath and to the left of the first stone. It represents how you are seeing your or your client's situation. It also highlights Freyja's magical cloak of "Persistence" and having a "fixed" focus in order to direct your intuition. Like Freyja shape-shifting and taking flight in the form of a falcon, allow your third-eye vision to soar high above and look into your client's world.

Rune 3: The position for the third stone is a couple of inches beneath and to the right of the first stone. It's linked with the "Direction," significant to the potential outcome of the situation in question. How "mutable" is the flow of the emotional energy and what changes may be necessary, if any? If there's stagnation, where is the energy stuck? Where is the energy going? What shows an answer or potential resolution to the question? Are any of Freyja's golden tears dropping in this trine of power?

Take a moment to contemplate the messages you are intuiting from the dialogue among the three stones. Do the correlations with these stones—their astrological, elemental, or archetypal affinities—offer additional insight into the dynamic forces interacting within the triangle?

The messages of all three stones should be considered in regard to the issues presented during the placement of the first sone. What are the three stones' singular message? What insights from the stones are most relevant for helping your client connect with a potential sense of a resolution or peace of mind?

Thor's Hammer: Five-Stone Rune Cast

Reputedly, the strongest of the Aesir gods was Thor, god of thunder. His magic hammer, the Mjolnir, considered one of the greatest wonders in Norse myths, could never be destroyed, yet it could destroy anything it struck. Its power was so great that in modern times its image is still being used as an amulet to protect one's hopes and encourage the weak to become strong.

For divinatory purposes, it calls on the ancient powers and shows how to cross the bridge between the conscious and subconscious mind and meet in the middle of the left and the right hemispheres of the brain. It can also help identify nonverbal truths, practical concerns, and one's unfolding evolution.

To do this rune cast, first contemplate your question or yearnings. You may want to call on Thor or Odin for guidance as how to best shuffle or toss your runes. Once your stones are placed on your table, let your stones inspire insights for unspoken questions and give you understanding of what needs to be discussed.

When divining with Thor's hammer, you have the opportunity to highlight your or your client's inner spirit, their emotions, ideas about their most important commitments, and hopes for their fulfillment. Look at the myths, planetary influences, and archetypes connected with each stone. How do their stories complement or condemn one another? What do your stones show you about what your client wants and their potential direction?

After you select a stone, position each one, starting at the bottom of the hammer's design. The first and second stones, which symbolize the mind and thought patterns, are the foundation of the hammer design. Then, place the third and fourth runes at the top of the hammer design. Once these four runes are placed, the fifth and final rune is placed in the center of the hammer, in the middle of the other runes. Once your runes are placed, you are ready to begin your reading.

Stone Positions

Rune 1: The Subconscious. This stone sits in the position that highlights what is hidden from view. It also offers clues about the underlying influences that may be influencing you or your client's situation.

Rune 2: The Conscious. This stone targets the issue to be discussed and your client's general concerns. It can indicate current obstacles that one is facing. What does the stone have to say regarding the influences depicted in the first rune? Does it increase or decrease the strength of the hammer?

Rune 3: The Superconscious. What is the hope for the future outcome of the situation being discussed? What beneficial forces are being called into action? What is this stone's most important message?

Rune 4: Action/Reaction. The rune that sits in this position represents the action that is needed to overcome any struggles. If you're familiar with a stone's astrological or archetypal correspondence, look for planetary clues to understand what kind of energy will help raise the power of Thor's mighty hammer.

Rune 5: Resolution or direction. This stone points to the potential direction Thor's hammer will ultimately take. It also can indicate what is needed to release any mounting pressure, win the battles in life, and achieve a positive outcome.

THE ZODIAC TWELVE-HOUSE CARD SPREAD AND WHEEL OF LIFE RUNE CAST

NOTE: Because the instructions for creating a Twelve House Zodiac Card Spread and Odin's Twelve-Stone Wheel of Life Rune Cast are the same, my discussion combines this information instead of repeating it.

To offer these readings, not only do you need to know how to discuss the messages and meanings in the cards or stones, but you also need to know how to discuss the meanings of the twelve zodiac houses. If you understand how to interpret the significance of the twelve houses, you can apply the meaning for each of the twelve-card or twelve-stone positions to create the underlying foundation for this reading. If you don't know the significance of each of the twelve houses on the zodiac wheel, practicing this layout will give you an opportunity to learn their significance.

Because this reading requires the discussion of twelve or more cards or stones, you need to allow more time for giving this type of reading than if you would be doing one with five or fewer stones or cards.

In your mind's eye, imagine the appearance of the zodiac wheel with the twelve houses arranged in consecutive order. Once you envision it, you might want to silently call on your muses or Odin to inspire your circle's message.

When it's time to create the layout for your card spread or rune cast, ask your oracle a personal question. If you or your client doesn't have a question, shuffle your cards or toss your stones and prepare to offer a general life reading. Select your twelve cards or stones and place them one by one counterclockwise in your imagined zodiac circle. Each card or stone that you select will represent one of the twelve houses in sequential order. Each will be discussed regarding the qualities of the house position where they sit. The first card or stone that you draw represents the first house, the second will concern the second house, your third draw is significant to the third house, and so on as you continue placing cards or stones in succession to reflect the activities of each of the twelve houses around the circle.

The positions of the twelve cards or stones for this twelve-house layout are identical to the descriptions of the twelve houses that were presented in chapter 1. If you aren't familiar with their significance, the planetary rulers of the houses, their elemental foundation, their polarities, and the aspects between them, you may want to review this information. Everything you know about the wheel of the zodiac and its houses can provide insight when you create zodiac spreads. Its layout positions are interpreted as follows.

Card or Stone Position	Zodiac Ruler	House Qualities
Position 1	Aries	One's self, ego, appearances, personality
Position 2	Taurus	Finances, material possessions & ambitions
Position 3	Gemini	Personal expression, communications
Position 4	Cancer	Home, family, security, mother
Position 5	Leo	Creativity, children, romantic affairs
Position 6	Virgo	Work, service, health, diet
Position 7	Libra	Partnerships, marriage, commitments
Position 8	Scorpio	Occult, taxes, death, others' finances
Position 9	Sagittarius	Philosophy, higher education, travel
Position 10	Capricorn	Career, reputation, aspirations
Position 11	Aquarius	Community, friends, associations
Position 12	Pisces	The subconscious, dreams, secrets

The twelve-house astrological rune cast. Each number represents a house on the zodiac wheel. Each randomly-selected stone is interpreted in relation to the house it sits within. For example, in this illustration, the rune Sigel, linked with the Sun, will be read in relation to its connections with the 1st house ruled by Mars, dominated by Aries.

Keep practicing this spread, and if you're consistent, you'll quickly advance on the high road to combining astrology, card readings, and rune readings. The more you analyze this layout, the more quickly your intuitive skills will advance. You can use this layout with either runestones or Tarot cards. Practical experience analyzing horoscopes will quicken your understanding of how to work with the zodiac card spreads and Odin's rune casts.

When you do a zodiac spread and someone pulls the Wheel of Fortune card, and it sits in the second house of finances and ambitions, you'll know that Jupiter, the planet influencing this card's meaning, will be blessing your client's road to their financial dreams. If someone selects the runestone Is, and it sits in the position of the seventh house of intimate relations, there's a good chance that you'll be discussing how to balance (the seventh house supports the scales of balance) the complexities of emotions with lunar influences.

The more times you invite these oracular arts into your life, the more comfortable you'll feel conversing with their silence. Trust your process and keep your sixth sense open to the light of lucky stars shining above you.

Reading a Horoscope with the Addition of Cards or Runes

Sometimes after doing a reading, your client will ask you to answer "just one more question." For example, let's imagine that you've created a twelve-card zodiac spread and then decide that you'd like to select more cards for additional insight into the potential resolution of your client's stated problem. Perhaps after you have created a zodiac layout to discuss the potential of a romance, you are asked one more question, such as "Will he be faithful to me?"

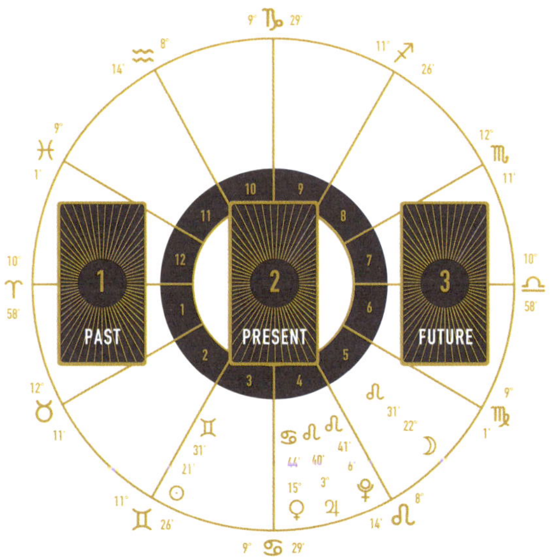

Astrological chart with three cards in center

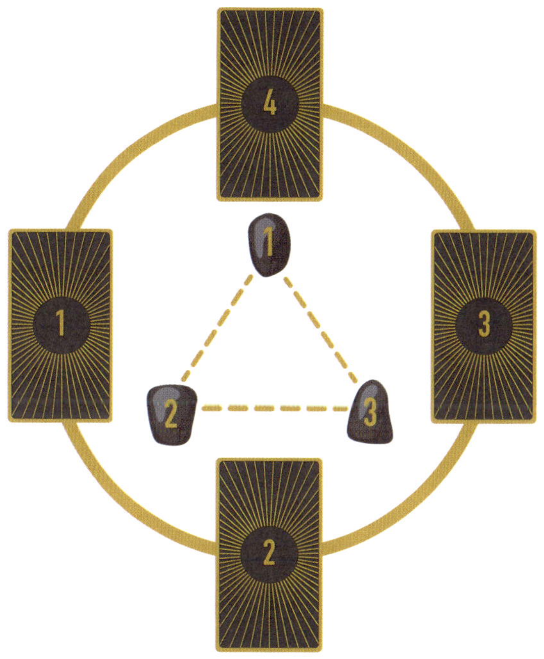

Runic trine in middle of Four-Card Cardinal Spread

If this occurs, you can create a three-card (or three-stone) layout and attach it to your zodiac card spread or rune cast if it feels more appropriate. Using both of these mediums in one layout creates a plethora of symbols to regard. As long as you're up for juggling multiple mediums, not only are these readings visually beautiful, but they offer exciting opportunities for storytelling. The outcome of combination astrology chart, stone, or card readings gives you an unmatchable, visual map of cosmic potentials, perspectives, and life purpose.

SAYING GOODBYE FOR NOW!

The more time you invite these mystic mediums into your life, the more comfortable you'll feel divining their messages. Keep a sense of adventure with each step you take on this journey, and keep your mind open to seeing the wisdom of the mystical eye shining on your path. Fast forward into the future, and if you continue to practice and play with these oracles, you'll be interpreting astrological charts, card spreads, and the casting of stones with evolving understanding and discerning insights. Wishing you much joy on your path!

APPENDIX 1

ZODIAC GUIDE FOR THE CARDS, STONES, AND ARCHETYPES

Astrology Signs

Sun Sign	Card	Rune	Archetype	Qualities
Aries	The Emperor	Tyr	Leader	Strong will, ambition, courage, independence
Taurus	High Priest	Ur	Shaman	Determination, fertility, stability, affection
Gemini	The Lovers	Eh	Messenger	Unity, communicating, choices, duality
Gemini	The Chariot	Eolh	Nurturer	Receptivity, protection, change, clairvoyance
Leo	Strength	Cen	Enchanter	Vitality, boldness, heroism, happiness
Virgo	The Hermit	Ger	Sage	Analyzing, finances, healing, wisdom
Libra	Justice	Gyfu	Diplomat	Balance, collaboration, fairness, mediating
Scorpio	Death	Eoh	Phoenix	Rebirth, transformation, the psychic, secretive
Sagittarius	Temperance	Rad	Teacher	Optimism, philosophy, expansion, travel
Capricorn	The Devil	Nyd	Authority	Finances, focus, responsibility, maturity
Aquarius	The Star	Mann	Reformer	Humanitarian, upbeat, empathy, freedom
Pisces	The Moon	Hoegl	Intuitive	Instinct, understanding, imagination, caring

Planets

Planet	Card	Rune	Archetype	Qualities
☉ Sun	The Sun	Sigel	The Self	Vitality, creativity, children, happiness
☽ Moon	The High Priestess	Is	Maiden	The feminine, esoterica, nurturing, dreams
Waxing moon	The High Priestess	Ethel	Maiden	Property, depth, memories, clairvoyance
Waning moon	The High Priestess	Thorn	Maiden	Challenge, oppression, taboo, travel
☿ Mercury	Magician	Os	Healer	Communication, travel, youthful, magic
♀ Venus	Empress	Beorc	Eros	Love, beauty, pleasure, happiness
♂ Mars	Tower	Feoh	Initiator	Action, confrontation, competition, autonomy
♃ Jupiter	Fortune	Wynn	Explorer	Expansion, foresight, positivity, winning
♄ Saturn	The World	Peordh	Wise Elder	Karma, values, responsibility, limits
♅ Uranus	The Fool	Daeg	The child	The unexpected, freedom, innovation, unrest
♆ Neptune	Hanged Man	Lagu	The Mystic	Dreams, illusion, intuition, nonconformity
♇ Pluto	Judgement	Ing	Rebirth	Transformation, disruption,

APPENDIX 2

OBTAINING YOUR NATAL CHART

If you already have your personal chart, great. If not, there are various available online sites that will create your chart(s) for little or no payment (some reports are for sale). You'll need to fill out a form and provide a birth date, time, and location of birth.

Within minutes you should obtain your birth or other charts. Look for a link on the home page that says *Free Horoscopes*.

For those of you wanting a chart, here are a couple of sites—if still online—that provide charts:

https://cafeastrology.com

https://Astro.com

As in any path of serious inquiry, your study of chart interpretation will be useful for developing expertise and learning to practice divination. In order to develop your skills, you may want to read Dusty Bunker's *The Beginner's Guide to Astrology* (REDFeather, 2017) or any other text that calls you to open its cover.

APPENDIX 3

JOURNAL TEMPLATE FOR RECORDING DIVINATION INSIGHTS

Date & Time

____

Today's Celestial Views

____

____

Tarot Insights

____

____

Rune Insights

____

____

Noteworthy Impressions
Type of reading I offered:

____

What oracle(s) did I use?

____

What key qualities were highlighted?

____

____

What did I discover?

____

____

What did I learn about my intuition?

____

____

ENDNOTES

INTRODUCTION

1. Kooch N. Daniels and Victor Daniels, *Tarot at a Crossroads: The Unexpected Meeting of Tarot and Psychology* (Atglen, PA: Schiffer, 2017), 252.

CHAPTER 1

1. A. T. Mann, *The Mandala Astrological Tarot* (San Francisco: Harper & Row, 1987), 22.

CHAPTER 3

1. Alan Oken, *As Above, So Below: A Primary Guide to Astrological Awareness* (New York: Bantam Books, 1973), 20.

CHAPTER 4

1. Paul Foster Case, *The Tarot: A Key to the Wisdom of the Ages* (Richmond, VA: Macoy, 1947), 123.

CHAPTER 5

1. Wikipedia contributors, "Runes," Wikipedia, the Free Encyclopedia, October 30, 2022.
2. Nigel Pennick, *Runic Astrology Starcraft and Timekeeping in the Northern Tradition* (Kent, UK: Aquarian, 1990), 50.

CHAPTER 6

1. C. G. Jung, *Man and His Symbols* (New York: Dell, 1968).
2. Daniels and Daniels, *Tarot at a Crossroads*.

BIBLIOGRAPHY

Amberstone, Ruth Ann, and Wald Amberstone. *Tarot Tips*. St. Paul, MN: Llewellyn, 2003.

Atwater, P. M. H. *The Magical Language of Runes*. Santa Fe, NM: Bear, 1986.

Blum, Ralph. *The Rune Cards: Ancient Wisdom for the New Millennium*. New York: St. Martin's, 1997.

Bolen, Jean Shinoda. *Goddesses in Every Woman: A New Psychology of Woman*. New York: Harper Perennial, 1984.

Burt, Kathleen. *Archetypes of the Zodiac*. St. Paul, MN: Llewellyn, 1988.

Case, Paul Foster. *The Tarot: A Key to the Wisdom of the Ages*. Richmond, VA: Macoy, 1947.

Cooper, Jason. *Using the Runes: A Comprehensive Introduction to the Art of Runecraft*. Northamptonshire, UK: Aquarian, 1986.

Crowley, Aleister. *The Book of Thoth: An Interpretation of the Tarot*. New York: Samuel Weiser, 1974.

Daniels, Kooch N. *Mystic Spirit Tarot Playbook*. Atglen, PA: Schiffer, 2020.

Daniels, Kooch N., and Victor Daniels. *Tarot at a Crossroads: The Unexpected Meeting of Tarot and Psychology*. Atglen, PA: Schiffer, 2017.

Daniels, Kooch N., and Victor Daniels. *Tarot d'Amour*. Newburyport, MA: Weiser, 2003.

Gilbert, Toni. *Gaining Archetypal Vision: A Guidebook for Using Archetypes in Personal Growth and Healing*. Atglen, PA: Schiffer, 2011.

Greer, Mary K. *Tarot Constellations: Patterns of Personal Destiny*. North Hollywood, CA: Newcastle, 1987.

Howard, Michael. *The Magic of the Runes: Their Origins and Occult Power*. Bungay, UK: Aquarian, 1980.

Jung, C. G. *Man and His Symbols*. New York: Dell, 1968.

Lewis, Ursual. *Chart Your Own Horoscope*. New York, Grosset & Dunlap, 1976.

Lucina, Juno. *The Alchemy of Tarot*. Atglen, PA: Schiffer, 2011.

Mann, A. T. *The Mandala Astrological Tarot*. San Francisco: Harper & Row, 1987.

Nevin, Bruce. *Astrology Inside Out: A New Approach to Astrology*. West Chester, PA: Whitford (c/o Schiffer), 1982.

Nicols, Sallie. *Jung and Tarot: An Archetypal Journey*. York Beach, ME: Weiser Books, 1991.

Oken, Alan. *As Above, So Below: A Primary Guide to Astrological Awareness*. New York: Bantam Books, 1973.

Pennick, Nigel. *Runic Astrology Starcraft and Timekeeping in the Northern Tradition*. Kent, UK: Aquarian, 1990.

Place, Robert. *Alchemy and the Tarot*. Saugerties, NY: Hermes, 2011.

Sephiroth, Jack, Allen Dempster, and Jaymi Elford. *Runic Tarot*. Torino, Italy: Lo Scarabeo, 2021.

Thorsson, Edred. *Futhark: A Handbook of Rune Magic*. York Beach, ME: Samuel Weiser, 1989.

Tyson, Donald. *Runic Astrology: Chart Interpretations through the Runes*. Woodbury, MN: Llewellyn, 1988.

Walker, Barbara. *The Woman's Encyclopedia of Myths and Secrets*. Edison, NJ: Castle Books, 1996.

Wanless, James. *Voyager Tarot: Way of the Great Oracle*. Carmel, CA: Merrill West, 1989.

Wells, James P. *Tarot for Manifestation: Use the Cards to Make Your Desires a Reality*. San Francisco: Tarot Media, 2011.

Wikipedia contributors. "Runes." Wikipedia, the Free Encyclopedia. October 30, 2022.

Willis, Tony. *The Runic Workbook: Understanding and Using the Power of Runes*. Northamptonshire, UK: Aquarian,1986.